The Tech Phoenix

T.N. Manoharan is currently a member of the RBI's Standing External Advisory Committee for evaluating applications for universal banks and small finance banks. He is also the chairman of IDBI Bank and is a member of the boards of Mahindra & Mahindra, Tech Mahindra and the National Bank for Financing Infrastructure and Development. He is a chartered accountant (CA) of 39 years' standing and a law graduate.

Manoharan was part of the government-nominated board for the revival of Satyam Computer Services Limited. He served as chairman of the committee on Accounting Standards and Taxation of the Confederation of Indian Industry during 2009–11 and was the president of the Institute of Chartered Accountants of India in 2006–07. He has authored books for professionals and students on taxation.

He has received several awards including the CNN-IBN 'Indian of the Year 2009' from the Prime Minister of India. He was awarded the Padma Shri on 7 April 2010.

V. Pattabhi Ram is an author, public speaker and teacher, besides being a CA. An alumnus of St. Joseph's College, Tiruchi, he interned at the audit house Deloitte. He has taught over 75,000 CA students and is a regular speaker at the professional seminars circuit. His books include *Ticking Times: An Accountant and a Gentleman*, a novel set in the backdrop of the audit profession; *A Few Good Men*, and *Nightingales: How Eleven Women Overcame Obstacles on the Road of Life*, both bio-sketches; *Building a Legacy*, a biography of A. Ramakrishna, the former deputy managing director of L&T, which was released by the Vice President of India. His book *First Lessons in Strategic Financial Management*, co-authored with S.D. Bala, is a popular textbook among CA students.

Praise for the Book

T.N. Manoharan is to be congratulated for writing this amazing book, which narrates an unprecedented team effort to turn around a company rich in multiple assets but with no money. As another insider, I can say that a group of six persons welded themselves into a single, integrated team to complete their task in 100 days. This book tells the story, true and factual. The author and his associate V. Pattabhi Ram are to be applauded.

—**Tarun Das**, Former Director General,
Confederation of Indian Industry

The Satyam resurrection is a unique story. The swift action by the government resulted in a turnaround in a record time of 100 days without infusion of taxpayers' money and in collaboration with a few good men of repute and expertise. I compliment Manoharan for documenting this remarkable story of corporate rescue. The book is truly an engrossing read.

—**Shyamala Gopinath**, Former Deputy Governor,
Reserve Bank of India

This event-by-event, crisis-by-crisis account of the saga of the then biggest corporate fraud in India reads like a thriller, where one is hooked onto the curiosity of 'what next?' Manoharan, who played a key role as a member of the government-appointed board to salvage Satyam after a billion-dollar financial fraud, has penned a page-turner that brings alive the drama of a globally unique rescue of the seemingly doomed IT giant. Though a dozen years have since passed, the contemporary relevance of many of the lessons from this episode have been brought out well by the author. These are supplemented by brief but deep generalizations, applicable not only to corporate governance but also in day-to-day life.

Written with minimal jargon and in a readable style, this is more than an insider's view; it is that of a person who was a saviour of Satyam. He also covers, with empathy and fairness, Ramalinga Raju's social ventures.

Apart from the deep analysis, the documents, research and detailed narration provide an invaluable record. This book is a *must-read* for all those interested in corporate governance, whether practitioners, academics, students or policymakers.

—**Kiran Karnik**, Former President, NASSCOM, and ex-Chair of the government-appointed board for Satyam

The Tech Phoenix: Satyam's 100-Day Turnaround is unique in the simplicity with which it lays out the facts and detailed mechanics of the fraud. The sharp accounting mind of the author shines through. However, equally fascinating is the very nuanced insight into the motivations, described as the Jekyll and Hyde of Raju. A must-read indeed!

—**Shikha Sharma**, Economist and Banker

T.N. Manoharan's book stands out for being a first-hand account of the revival story of Satyam. Having worked closely together as members of the government-constituted board to salvage the company, I can vouch that Manoharan's narrative is honest and genuine. Satyam's 100-day turnaround success was about doing whatever it takes to restore the nation's credibility internationally. The key takeaway is recognizing India's deep strength when the government and the private sector work as one for the common good.

—**Deepak Parekh**, Chairman, HDFC Limited

The Satyam experience is truly like the word 'satyam'—discovering what the truth really was. The key was how regulators, bankers and directors worked together to secure and enhance the value of Satyam and protected the interests of all stakeholders with a long-term perspective in mind. It was an admirable collaborative effort and a watershed event for corporate India.

—**Suneeta Reddy**, Managing Director, Apollo Hospitals Group

The Tech Phoenix

SATYAM'S
100-DAY TURNAROUND

T. N. MANOHARAN
and **V. PATTABHI RAM**

RUPA

First published by
Rupa Publications India Pvt. Ltd 2022
7/16, Ansari Road, Daryaganj
New Delhi 110002

Sales Centres:

Allahabad Bengaluru Chennai
Hyderabad Jaipur Kathmandu
Kolkata Mumbai

Copyright © T.N. Manoharan and V. Pattabhi Ram 2022

The views and opinions expressed in this book are the authors' own and the facts are as reported by them which have been verified to the extent possible, and the publishers are not in any way liable for the same.

All rights reserved.
No part of this publication may be reproduced, transmitted, or stored in a retrieval system, in any form or by any means, electronic, mechanical, photocopying, recording or otherwise, without the prior permission of the publisher.

P-ISBN: 978-93-5520-822-4
E-ISBN: 978-93-5520-823-1

First impression 2022

10 9 8 7 6 5 4 3 2 1

The moral right of the authors has been asserted.

Printed in India

This book is sold subject to the condition that it shall not, by way of trade or otherwise, be lent, resold, hired out, or otherwise circulated, without the publisher's prior consent, in any form of binding or cover other than that in which it is published.

We salute all Satyamites who helped us—the government-nominated board—fight the crisis and bring the business back on track

CONTENTS

How We Revived Satyam	*x*
Foreword by Anand Mahindra	*xvii*
Preface by T.N. Manoharan	*xxi*
Prologue	*xxv*

PART 1: THE CRASH

1.	The Scam Is Revealed	3
2.	Satyam Gets a New Board	9

PART 2: INSIDE SATYAM

3.	Testing the Waters	29
4.	Mitigation Measures	38

PART 3: JANUS-FACED

5.	'Edward Hyde' at Satyam	53
6.	Dr Henry Jekyll to the World	65

PART 4: RESCUE BEGINS

7.	Strategy and Funding	77
8.	Navigating Through Turbulence	96
9.	Satyam's SWOT	108

PART 5: HOW WE DID IT

10. Rejuvenating Employees — 127

11. Synergy with Customers — 136

12. Managing Money Without Defaults — 144

PART 6: SELECTING THE INVESTOR

13. Pre-Bid Approvals and Mediation — 153

14. Swayamvaram — 161

15. The Winner — 170

PART 7: TAKEAWAYS

16. Legislation and Governance — 185

17. Learnings for Life — 195

PART 8: THE DENOUEMENT

18. Award and Epilogue — 211

Acknowledgements — 221

List of Abbreviations — 222

Index — 225

HOW WE REVIVED SATYAM

1987 Satyam incorporated as Private Limited Co. — Jun 24

1991 Satyam goes public. — Aug 26

2008 The board meeting that precipitated the fall. — Dec 16

2009 Raju confesses. — Jan 07

Anurag Goel speaks to prospective board members. SEBI launches formal investigation. RoC seizes books and documents from Satyam's offices. — Jan 08

CLB suspends old board. — Jan 09

Government announces the first set of new board members. — Jan 11

Board meeting at Hyderabad. Kiran Karnik chairs. — Jan 12

PW informs that its audit reports are now unreliable. — Jan 13

Government announces a second set of board members including LIC-nominee S.B. Mainak. — Jan 15

Jan 17 — Board meeting at Hyderabad. Deepak Parekh chairs. Legal advisors and internal auditors appointed.

Jan 18 — SOS from leadership team. Forensic auditors appointed.

Jan 22&23 — Board meeting at Hyderabad. Tarun Das chairs. Discussion on continuity issues and way forward.

Jan 23 — A petition filed before SEBI for immunity.

Jan 26 — Strategy meeting at Hyderabad.

Jan 27 — Board meeting at Hyderabad.  T.N. Manoharan chairs. BCG appointed. Investment bankers appointed.

Jan 28 — A petition filed before the CLB for immunity. Loan sanctioned by IDBI and BoB.

Jan 29-31 — CLB grants immunity. Manoharan visits Bahrain.

Feb 02 — SEBI advises amendment to Takeover Code.

Feb 04&05 — Board meeting at Hyderabad.  C. Achuthan chairs. A.S. Murthy appointed as CEO. Homi Khusrokhan and Partho Datta appointed as special advisors.

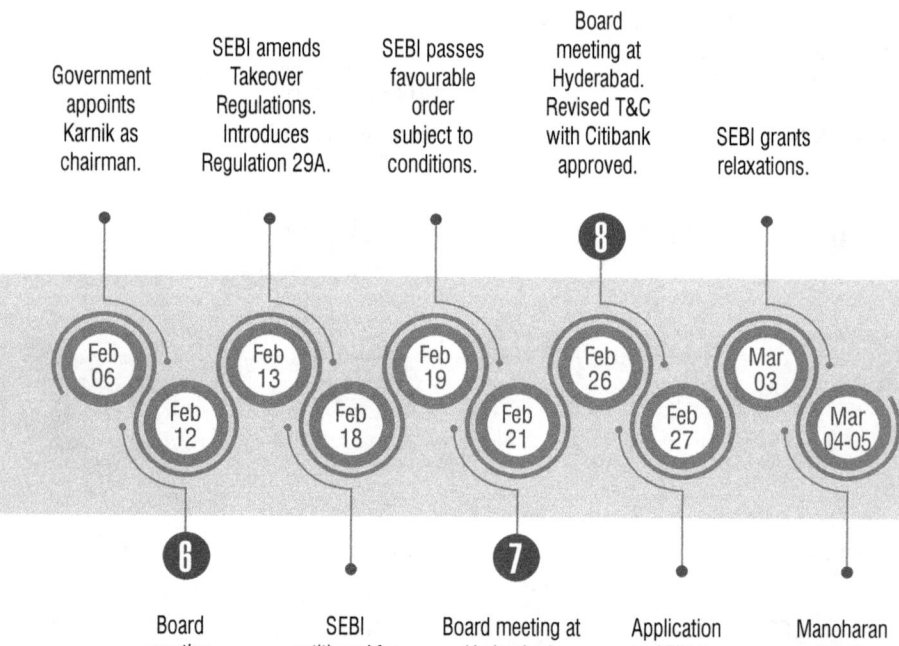

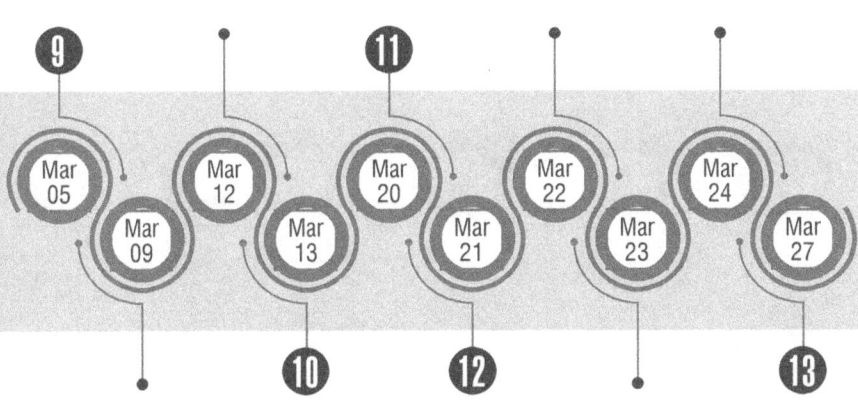

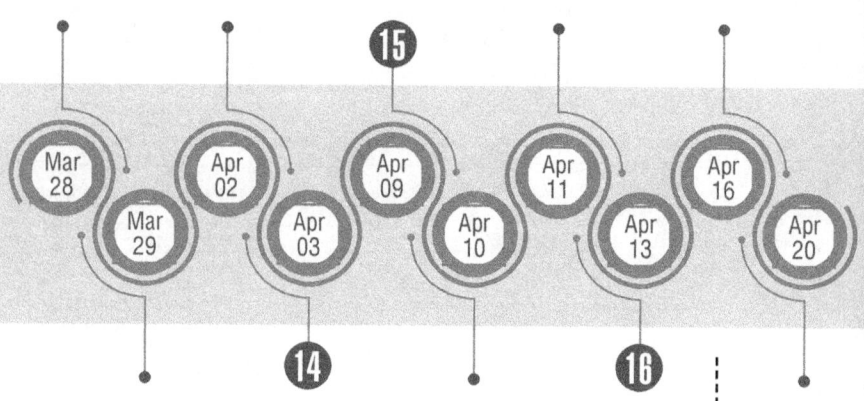

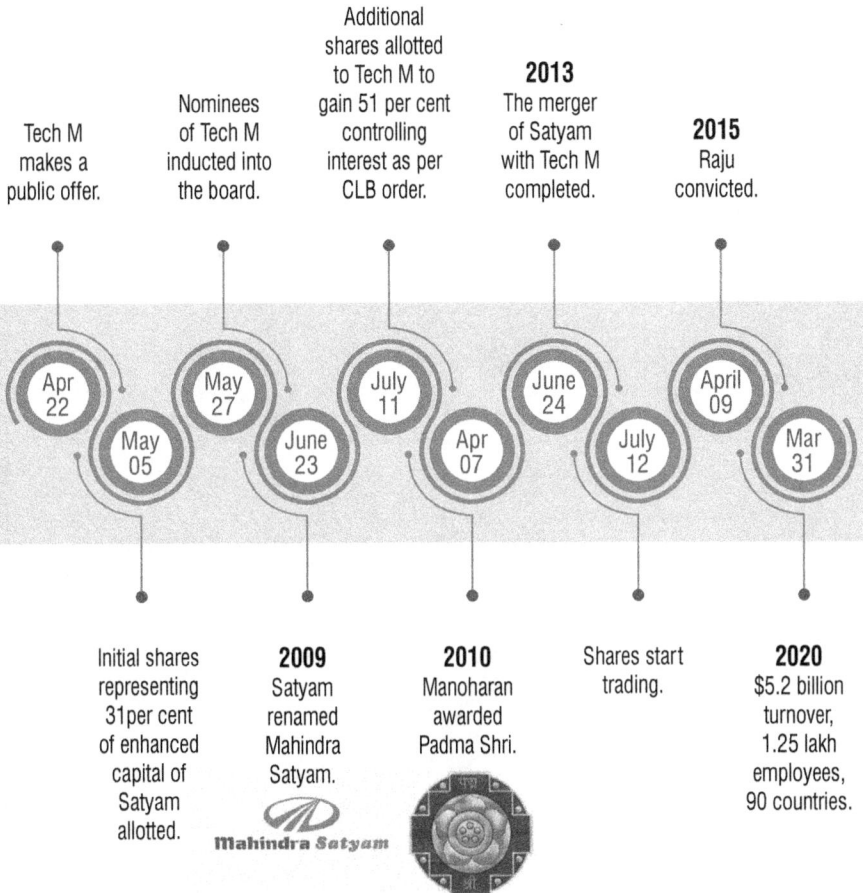

FOREWORD

When I first heard the news of Ramalinga Raju's confession in January 2009, I was taken aback. After all, Satyam, in the 1990s and 2000s, was a remarkable success story that showcased India's capability. The consequences of that one communication were enormous for all stakeholders. It would also affect India's image as a global provider of tech solutions.

However, the dire fallout that everyone was expecting did not come to pass. In the days that followed, I watched the happenings at Satyam with close interest as the government, through its nominated directors, arrested a losing cause. The government-nominated board members like Tarun Das, Deepak Parekh and Kiran Karnik were prominent and respected names in industry circles. Of course, T.N. Manoharan was a past president of the Institute of Chartered Accountants of India (ICAI) and C. Achuthan a legal eagle. And the largest investor—Life Insurance Corporation of India (LIC)—had in S. Balakrishna Mainak a nominee on the board as well. This board took rapid and decisive action to save the company, its employees and shareholders.

When the call for a strategic investor came, we at Mahindra brainstormed to see if there was a deal for us. It was an opportunity to grow inorganically, leapfrog in the ranking sweepstake and diversify within the technology space. More importantly, we wanted to explore the possibility of joining the mission of the government to resurrect Satyam and restore the faith of stakeholders. The board and its involvements inspired confidence in us. We saw a bargain, and it was essential to put our money to back the deal. This led to the decision to acquire Satyam, despite the bad reputation it had earned.

I remember well the first time I met Manoharan. It was clear that he was a man of few words. He would seldom speak, but when he did, he captured the attention of the room. His reputation preceded him because it was well known that he was doing the heavy lifting—in terms of groundwork—for the turnaround of the company and its sale to the new owners. That is why we felt it would be critical to request him to stay on the board once we completed the acquisition.

After that, the journey has been fabulous for us, and I am happy that our group played an essential role in a national cause.

In the ensuing years, I got to see Manoharan at much closer quarters. He is modest and self-effacing. But, over time, more varied aspects of his personality emerged. While the depth of his knowledge is singular, I also learnt about his enjoyment of various passions and pursuits—he is a marathon runner, for instance. He has a great sense of humour and, if drawn out, has a repository of witty anecdotes with which he regales us at board meetings.

Over time, he has become someone we all at the board are proud to call a friend.

He is perhaps the most suitable person to write about the happenings during those calamitous 100 days. He has been there, seen and done it all. This should be the most authoritative document on the subject, given his legal mind and attention to detail.

Today, those events of 13 years back might be blurred in everyone's memory or seem romantic, but it was a trial by fire. I appreciate that, instead of delving into Satyam's past and its fall, the book focusses on the turnaround during those 100 days. This story makes for a great case study in corporate turnaround and must be read in board rooms by corporate executives and B-school students.

I believe posterity should be told about the dramatic rescue operation because it echoes the spirit of 'Yes We Can'. We tend to forget a few things with time, but we cannot afford to ignore this one.

Anand Mahindra
Chairman, Mahindra Group
September 2022

PREFACE

When I stepped into Satyam in the winter of 2009, I had no idea how we would revive the company. All I knew was we would do it, come what may. I even told myself I would devote my every minute to Satyam. In hindsight, the faith was energizing. If someone had then told me it would take just 100 days, I would have laughed. The crisis was deep; I had no previous experience, and even India was embarking on this experiment for the first time. But the presence of Deepak Parekh, Kiran Karnik, Tarun Das and C. Achuthan on the team gave me and everyone else enormous trust and confidence.

Those 100 days were priceless education for me. During that period, I saw from close quarters the sorrow people go through when they are on the verge of losing a job. I also saw how a wounded lion can fight back in the corporate jungle. To me, it was an important engagement as my country's reputation was at stake. And the fact that the government chose me as one of the warriors to battle this added to my responsibility. I was, of course, extremely thankful that the government nominated on the board remarkable men with impeccable integrity and honour to make the turnaround happen.

When I turn up at meetings and conferences, I make it a point to jot things down. To me, journaling is second nature. I journaled about the Satyam events, and these entries became the basis of writing this book. Some may say this book is late by several years. But then, it is the only one written from first-hand experience and that too by an insider with a ringside view. There is a lot that corporate executives, bankers, regulators, management graduates and others who either have the urge to learn about a turnaround strategy or have a sense of history can pick up from this live case study.

The underpinning of the Satyam story is that if a nation makes up its mind and works with sagacity and maturity, it can achieve what it sets forth to do. Remember, at that time, the cradle of capitalism, the United States (US), used taxpayers' money to bail out collapsing giants in the wake of the global financial crisis. In contrast, India embarked on a public–private partnership that saw the most extraordinary corporate turnaround in history in the shortest time, without the government spending a rupee from its coffers.

Right after the successful turnaround of Satyam, I was invited by many forums in India and overseas, including a few renowned business schools from the US, the United Kingdom (UK), Australia, Singapore and the Middle East, to share my experience. There were suggestions in every such programme that I should publish my experience. Friends and well-wishers, too, agreed. Some even commented that there is a movie in this. But subsequent responsibilities kept me busy. Ultimately, I decided I must work on this project. I also felt that it was my duty to document the concerted effort of the country, the government and Satyamites to overcome what was corporate India's darkest period.

I am convinced the story must be told because it tells us about the art of the possible in times of failure. It must be said lest this remarkable period becomes just a blip in history.

Sometime in September 2020, I handed over my draft to Pattabhi Ram.

The lockdown caused by the pandemic, in a way, came in handy. Between 1 October and 14 December 2020, Pattabhi Ram and I had a series of online discussions, and in the space of those 75 days, came out with a readable story. After that, it went through multiple iterations, following readings by friends, a few Satyam associates, a few members of the Tech Mahindra group, journalists, veterans, some fresh out of college and a few college-goers.

In addition to sharing my experience, I have added two chapters to share my learnings: one from the corporate angle and another from a human life perspective. These, I am confident, will provide several takeaways for assimilation by the readers.

Happy reading.

T.N. Manoharan

PROLOGUE

26 November 2008, Mumbai

The day was running its course like any usual Wednesday. But as the clock chimed 30 minutes past nine, Maximum City froze.

Two gunmen entered Chhatrapati Shivaji Terminus, the heart of Mumbai's city-transport constellation, and opened fire, killing hundreds of unsuspecting citizens. The historic railway station, an example of Victorian Gothic architecture, turned chaotic as passengers ran helter-skelter for cover.

Moments later, an unbelieving world saw the Taj Mahal Palace hotel in Colaba begin to go up in smoke. Several explosions were heard across the hotel. Similar reports of mayhem flowed in from Cama Hospital, The Oberoi Trident and Leopold Cafe. Lashkar-e-Taiba, an international terror outfit, carried out a series of coordinated shoot-outs and bombings that shocked people.

Mumbai lay under the siege of madmen, and India was furious.

Prime Minister Manmohan Singh seethed with rage.[1] For once, Opposition Leader L.K. Advani was on the same page. The elite National Security Guard flew down from the national capital to fight the terrorists. After three days of intense conflict, by 29 November, the place had been sanitized, and the battle won.

---

[1] 'No Restrain in Case of Second 26/11: Manmohan Singh Told Hillary Clinton in 2009', *The Economic Times*, 10 June 2014, https://bit.ly/3oI8zBh. Accessed on 1 August 2022.

The incident was unprecedented and shook the country to the core. But it also showcased India's potential to tackle a crisis head-on and move ahead, instead of succumbing, getting numbed and paralysed to shocks.

All these elements would be present in the Satyam story, which began in the same year. It's that story that this book narrates.

PART 1

THE CRASH

1
THE SCAM IS REVEALED

7 January 2009, multiple cities

Like every other day, I woke up at 5 a.m., got into my tracksuit and reached Marina Beach. It is the world's second-largest beach after the one in Rio De Janeiro—Praia do Cassino.

That day, the weather was excellent and the breeze pleasing. The waves repeatedly touched the shores and retreated in a lazy rhythm. I saw men venture into the sea for fishing and ships anchored deep. A few morning walkers were busy feeding pigeons. At frequent intervals, flights descended towards the Chennai Airport for landing.

If jogging on the sand was physically exhausting, running closer to the sea where the sand is wet (stiff and tight) was pure joy. As I ran the 5.5-kilometre stretch from Lighthouse to Anna Memorial and back, my mind found the clarity to think through solutions to a few complicated problems. Little did I know then that I would, for the next several weeks, camp in the Nizam city of Hyderabad on a government mission, missing this opportunity to jog on the Marina! But as I will tell you soon, it was worth missing.

A few hours later, I was in my office. My usually clear desk was cluttered as I tried to gather inputs for a presentation.

A ticker appeared on the chat box. '₹5,000 crore fraud in Satyam. Raju steps down.'

I hastily typed, 'Oh my God! Any proof?'

My friend wrote, 'Give me a few seconds.'

In those few seconds, as time froze for me, I stared at the computer. I couldn't believe that this man, who once sat next to the US president in a public function, cooked the books.[1]

The proof came as an email attachment. It was a complete story of confession, now famous as the 'riding-a-tiger' letter, from the man who built Satyam into a shining star of the outsourcing business. I read with shock and disbelief.

At around 9.45 a.m., India's market regulator, the Securities and Exchange Board of India (SEBI), had a heart-stopping moment. Its head, Chandrashekhar Bhave, received this very same explosive mail from the chairman of Satyam Computer Services Limited, Byrraju Ramalinga Raju. In that letter, addressed to the Satyam board of directors, copied to SEBI and the stock exchanges, Raju made a stunning disclosure. The man revered as God in his native state of Andhra Pradesh[2] said he had falsified the company's books of accounts for several years. A stunned National Stock Exchange (NSE) called up Company Secretary G. Jayaraman to check if the content was correct. At 10.53 a.m., the confirmation of the mail's genuineness was faxed with the company's stamp affixed. There were repercussions across the world as incredulity slowly gave way to acceptance of reality.

An hour later, a series of phone calls were made across the world. In a motel in Frankfurt, Germany, a Satyam employee woke up following the telephone's persistent ring. It was 7.30 a.m., Central European Time. The room's curtains had been drawn, and it was snowing outside.

'Good morning, Sir. This is from the hotel's front desk.

---

[1]'Ramalinga Raju: From Brushing Shoulders with Bill Clinton to Prison Cell', NDTV, 9 April 2015, https://bit.ly/3Rfw7uC. Accessed on 5 July 2022.
[2]Tripathy, Devidutta, 'Roses, Posters, Prayers for Jailed Satyam Chief', Reuters, 15 January 2009, https://reut.rs/3NJsNVv. Accessed on 5 July 2022.

Kindly make alternative payment arrangements, or you will have to check out by noon.'

'What?'

'Kindly make alternative payment arrangements, or you will have to check out by noon.'

'But why?'

'Your credit card has been deactivated.'

'How come?' He just didn't understand what she was saying.

'Sir, switch on CNN-IBN. You will have all the details.'

The man dragged himself to pick the remote and half stupefied punched the numbers.

On the screen appeared the story of Ramalinga Raju's daring heist. Till now, in history, frauds had either been detected or whistle-blown. For perhaps the first time, a perpetrator was singing voluntarily. Till now, the world over, an investigation had led to a confession. For the first time, an admission would lead to an inquiry.

Several such calls were made in different parts of Europe and Australia. Some hotel guests frantically reached out to customers for help for making payments to the hotel or for making alternative accommodations, and a few walked the distance to their workplace to seek shelter. India's credibility was on the line. Had the information technology (IT) sector, the darling of the masses, turned rogue? The revelation jolted corporate India, the Indian middle class and the rest of the world. By evening, it was clear the emerging scandal would hit every stakeholder—investors, employees, customers, bankers and regulators—big time.

The repercussions were swift.

In Dalal Street, the nerve centre of India's equity market, the Satyam stock fell like ninepins. Investors, who once paid fancy prices to acquire the shares in secondary market operations and initial public offerings, both in India and abroad, now felt betrayed. By the end of the day, the scrip dropped by almost

80 per cent, cleaning up billions of rupees worth of investors' wealth.

A year ago, in January 2008, Satyam quoted ₹541. On 6 January 2009, you could have bought a Satyam share on the NSE at ₹178.20.[3] On 9 January 2009, the share traded at ₹11.50 on the Bombay Stock Exchange (BSE) and ₹6.50 on the NSE.[4] What a fall! A professor of corporate finance and capital market, teaching a class that day, told his students not to touch Satyam even with a bargepole.

Worse followed.

Employees were shattered psychologically and financially. The prospects of getting a salary for the first month of the new year seemed bleak, and the possibility of becoming unemployed looked real. The fact that in 2008, there wasn't much recruitment on campuses added to the dismal scenario.[5]

A few top leaders of Satyam working in various geographies were angry. Their effort and sweat in building the company had gone down the tube. They worried about their personal image getting tarnished and wanted to leave the company.

Customers were concerned about the continuity of projects executed by Satyam. There was every probability of the need to migrate to an expensive competitor as Satyam's future looked dim. Many hesitated to pay the company its dues. Worse still, some customers turned anxious about a possible setback in their brand image if they continued associating with a 'tainted' organization and so wished to step out. There was a genuine fear that Satyam may become an international outcaste.

The US Securities and Exchange Commission (SEC)

---

[3]Retrieved from NSE data on Satyam Computers.
[4]Bhatt, Sheela, 'Demand to Reverse all Satyam Share Deals of Jan 7', Rediff, 9 January 2009, https://bit.ly/3vy9FU3. Accessed on 1 August 2022.
[5]Bhosale, Jayashree, 'IT, Core Manufacturing Sectors Skip 2008–2009 Campus Placements', *The Economic Times*, 7 September 2009, https://bit.ly/3NS94CW. Accessed on 7 July 2022.

geared itself to initiate action as Satyam was listed on the New York Stock Exchange (NYSE). So did the regulators in India, particularly the Ministry of Corporate Affairs (MCA) and SEBI. The Indian government seriously considered the fallout of India's image in the international marketplace. Coming close on the heels of the global financial crisis of 2008, which the country had smartly sidestepped, it was terrible news.

India was angry—very, very angry.

And then, in the next 100 days, by 16 April 2009, the place had been sanitized, and the war won. On the same day, the nation went to the polls.

This is the story of those dramatic 100 days, when the Indian government, in an unprecedented public–private partnership, masterminded the most remarkable turnaround in corporate history.

And as a board member, I was a part of the transformation; it was an act that later got me the Padma Shri. In the board were Kiran Karnik, Deepak Parekh, Tarun Das, C. Achuthan and S. Balakrishna Mainak.

> **WEAVING WOOL**
>
> Satyam's financial results took everyone for a ride: the analysts, the investors, the regulators and those who gave away awards.
>
> The results hoodwinked the regulators and investors as Satyam fudged numbers to announce profits that met or surpassed analysts' expectations. And irrespective of the industry's performance, the company consistently posted a net margin above 20 per cent quarter after quarter. Analysts praised Ramalinga Raju's vision, and organizations feted him with awards. For example, in 2007, Ernst & Young named Raju the 'Entrepreneur of the Year'. Meanwhile, The Institute of Internal Auditors, USA, gave the 'Recognition of Commitment Award' to Satyam's internal audit team. Microsoft announced Satyam as 'Citizenship Partner of the Year', and Computer Associates gave the 'Vision, Impact, Progress Award, 2007' to Raju's company.
>
> A year later, in 2008, Satyam won the 'Golden Peacock Global Award' for excellence in corporate governance. Once the scam broke out, the UK-based World Council for Corporate Governance took it back. The same year, it won the 'SAP Pinnacle Award' under the 'Service—Ecosystem Expansion (Growth)' category! Today, the irony stares us in the face.
>
> Clearly, the organizers had no clue about the hidden truth.

2

SATYAM GETS A NEW BOARD

Within minutes of receiving Ramalinga Raju's astonishing mail, Chandrashekhar Bhave swung into action. So did Prem Chand Gupta.

Bhave, a former 1975 batch Indian Administrative Service (IAS) officer and a qualified electrical engineer, was the chairman of SEBI. His years of experience as a regulator had taught him that Raju's confession could potentially destroy the market. Fifty-eight-year-old Gupta was the country's minister for corporate affairs. A consummate politician, he knew that if not handled well, the event would blow up in the government's face.

On 8 January, SEBI announced a formal investigation into the circumstances surrounding the financial irregularities alleged in Raju's letter.

Meanwhile, the Prime Minister's Office (PMO) wanted the MCA to take charge of the situation. Acting immediately, the ministry asked industry doyen Som Mittal, the then president of the non-profit organization National Association of Software and Service Companies (NASSCOM), to fly to Hyderabad, understand the crisis and file a first-person report. In the city that is home to the Charminar, Mittal met Satyam's orphaned leadership team, held a discussion with them and later debriefed the MCA. What followed in the national capital was a series of back-to-back meetings, after which New Delhi identified three options with which to handle this extraordinary situation.

One, let the market decide the fate of Satyam Computers. Two, devise a bailout plan and infuse funds into the company. And three, think out of the box to come out with a unique plan of action.

Plan A, namely to allow market forces to decide Satyam's fate, was among the best traditions of capitalism. The US, home to the market economy, did precisely that when Lehman Brothers crashed. In 2008, the 158-year-old investment-banking firm filed for bankruptcy following the global financial crisis. The Bush government did not blink as it let Lehman die.

Should India do to the technology major what the US did to an investment bank? The consensus view was, 'No, Satyam is a different cup of tea.' The argument went thus: India was being showcased as an attractive destination for international investors. The IT sector had helped place the country prominently on the world map. If Satyam, listed overseas, was allowed to crumble, it would affect the inflow of foreign investments. Unless deftly handled, this episode might hamper India's reputation globally and hinder its brand. Moreover, Satyam's annual report declared over 650 clients, of which 185 were listed among the Fortune 500. A headless Satyam could send the wrong signals. This situation needed quick action, and only the government was best equipped to act that fast.

There were other concerns as well about Plan A. These had to do with employees, customers, investors and vendors, among others. Technology companies had not made significant job offers the previous year, and thus, the job market was not lively. Incidentally, many fresh IT recruits had not been sent joining letters.[1] If Satyam was allowed to go down the tube, many of its employees, barring a few, would add to the growing number

---

[1]Mohandas, Poornima, 'Tech Firms Start to Pull Back on Hires', *Mint*, 11 July 2008, https://bit.ly/3bRYIWu. Accessed on 7 July 2022.

of unemployed IT professionals. This could prove awkward for the government as India's global image of being a preferred destination for process outsourcing would suffer.

Investors were not going to be sympathetic. In all likelihood, those in the US would move class-action suits that could severely impact Satyam. In a class-action suit, several people with similar injuries caused by the same person jointly go to the court for compensation. This act is to protect the interest of people who are geographically spread out and also to avoid multiple litigations. Previous examples of these suits were fresh in everyone's memory. For instance, when Enron went bankrupt, investors received a considerable settlement in 2002. At $7.2 billion, it was the largest equity class-action deal in history.[2] When WorldCom happened, investors cashed nearly $6.2 billion in lawsuits.[3] As the later months proved, Satyam's apprehension was not misplaced. In 2011, the company paid $125 million to settle US-shareholder litigation.[4]

Vendors and service providers could terminate contracts and make claims on Satyam's assets for recovering dues. Government agencies, and in particular the tax department, might freeze bank accounts and attach properties for potential demands to be collected under various laws. This could kill any chances of revival. Most importantly, corporate India would suffer a massive loss of face. This would lead to reluctance among foreign players to invest in or do business with Indian companies.

In short, employees could lose their jobs, investors might file class-action suits, vendors and customers might terminate contracts and the image of corporate India could take a beating

---

[2]Hays, Kristen, 'Enron Settlement: $7.2 Billion to Shareholders', *Chron.*, 9 September 2008, https://bit.ly/3blw0NG. Accessed on 1 August 2022.
[3]'In re WorldCom, Inc. Securities Litigation', Bernstein Litowitz, Berger & Grossman LLP, https://bit.ly/3Ii8qO5. Accessed on 7 July 2022.
[4]'Mahindra Satyam Settles US Law Suits for $125 m', *The Hindu BusinessLine*, 13 March 2018, https://bit.ly/3OQwVn7. Accessed on 1 August 2022.

abroad. The threat was real, stark and naked. No government could afford to let this happen. So, Plan A, of allowing market forces to decide, did not find favour.

Plan B was for the government to put in money. This proposition was risky, as the ruling party could be accused of abusing taxpayers' money to rescue a private player. India was three months shy of national elections, and a bailout could drag the ruling party into a needless political controversy. It could even set a wrong precedent for when such frauds reoccurred.

Therefore, the government had to think out of the box to find a third route, shelving the two popular options. Thus, it settled on Plan C, namely superseding the existing board and constituting a new team made up of government nominees drawn from various fields. It was a public–private partnership to safeguard stakeholders' interests and redeem India's image globally. The appointment of a new board would be the first step in that direction. Later, this step was considered a masterstroke, and the 100-day journey to recovery was a global case study in handling a crisis.

On the same 8 January, armed with a court order, Henry Richard, the Registrar of Companies (RoC), Andhra Pradesh, headed to Satyam's registered office at the Mayfair Trade Centre, S.P. Road, Secunderabad, to seize its statutory documents and electronic records. His next search was at Bahadurpally, where Satyam's central server for accounts was kept. The work continued into the wee hours of the next morning, after which Richard arrived at the Satyam office in My Home Hub in Hi-Tech City. Simultaneously, his colleagues moved to other locations where the IT records were kept. By late evening, on 9 January, the RoC and his team had completed their task. It had taken them 24 hours to carry out the whistle-stop tour.

In Hyderabad alone, Satyam had 19 offices, which were during the next one year pruned down to three locations.

But we are getting ahead of the story.

◆

Three weeks earlier, in a boardroom in Hyderabad, Satyam Computers set in motion a chain of events, which would eventually lead to its fall. This meeting would afterwards become an albatross around the neck of the independent directors.[5]

Satyam Infocity
16 December 2008
2.00 p.m. IST

Both Chairman Ramalinga Raju and his brother Managing Director Rama Raju had done their homework. They turned to a long-time associate, whole-time director Ram Mynampati, for support. This was an important board meeting, and as subsequent events showed, this was the duo's last board meeting of the company they had founded 21 years ago.

One of the agenda items for that day was Satyam's acquisition of two of Raju's family businesses: Maytas Infra and Maytas Properties. These limited liability companies were involved in infrastructure activity and had even bagged a few government contracts. As interested parties, the brothers stayed away from the discussion, and the board elected the dean of the Indian School of Business (ISB), Professor M. Rammohan Rao, to the chair.

The two Raju brothers, academic Dr Mangalam Srinivasan, civil servant T.R. Prasad, Indian Institute of Technology (IIT) Delhi director Prof. V.S. Raju and Mynampati were present in person. Indian-American Dr Krishna Palepu and the father of the Pentium chip, Vinod Dham, joined via audio.

Chief Financial Officer (CFO) Srinivas Vadlamani,

---

[5]The following details are drawn from the minutes of this board meeting.

Company Secretary G. Jayaraman and Head of Mergers and Acquisitions (M&A) Srinivasu Satti checked in as special invitees. Including Prof. Rao, 12 people were present at the ill-fated meeting.

Rao requested Mynampati and others in the management team to explain why these acquisitions should take place and how the valuations were done. After all, these businesses were in uncharted territory and unrelated to Satyam's core competency.

Mynampati had come prepared. He outlined the prevailing scenario in outsourcing markets and explained why it made sense to diversify. The economy, he argued, lay in a glorious mess. It would be tough to achieve rapid growth in the next two years. There were pressures on margins, and foreign exchange (forex) rates were both volatile and unpredictable. He pointed out that 95 per cent of Satyam's clients were from developed markets and that these countries were hit by the global financial crisis. Worse still, discomfort around the US government's outsourcing views existed. Mynampati wound up suggesting that it was time to de-risk the company through diversification.

Next, the CFO took over. Vadlamani informed the board that Maytas Infra was valued based on SEBI regulations, and Ernst & Young had assessed Maytas Properties.

The M&A head, Srinivasu Satti, talked about why it did not make sense to acquire IT assets, and how, in emerging economies, the role of hard infrastructure was critical. He spoke of business opportunities in China and India, and how governments worldwide were backing infrastructure spending to ward off unemployment, create spending cycles and aid economic growth. He pitched for diversification into infrastructure.

The consideration for Maytas Infra was placed at ₹1,504 crore ($307 million) and for Maytas Properties at ₹6,410 crore

($1,308 million). Together, these numbers added up to ₹7,914 crore ($1,615 million).

Vadlamani told the board that Maytas Properties had a land bank of 6,800 acres and could construct 245 million square feet of space. This was almost one-third of DLF's properties, whereas the valuation was one-tenth of DLF's valuation. He remarked that Luthra & Luthra (L&L Partners), the Delhi-based law firm, had done their due diligence of the title to the properties.

On the valuation of Maytas Infra, the CFO said that against the market price of ₹490 per share, the acquisition of a 31 per cent stake from the promoters would be at ₹475 per share. Another 20 per cent stake would be acquired from the public through an open offer at ₹525 per share. Thus, the consideration for the 51 per cent stake totalled at ₹1,504 crore.

The board's consent was also sought to invest up to ₹6,410 crore for acquiring Maytas Properties as a wholly owned subsidiary, at a share price to be fixed by valuation experts. The acquisition would be funded partly by internal accruals[6] (75 per cent) and partly through borrowing (25 per cent). Vadlamani requested the members to authorize the company to borrow funds from various banks and financial institutions on occasion.

It was now time for the board members to offer their views. Dr Srinivasan, who had been with the company since 1991, wondered if Satyam had any specific reasons, external or otherwise, for this initiative. She was sceptical about its timing and asked, 'Why now?'

Mynampati informed the board that Satyam faced a takeover threat by unwanted suitors at unattractive prices.

---

[6]These represent profits retained with the company. When a company earns profits, it pays out a part of it as dividends and retains the balance. This is called reserves or internal accruals in accounting language.

Did Dr Srinivasan smell a rat? Alas, we will never know. She was either offended that the board hadn't been consulted earlier, had suspicions of wrongdoing or perhaps both. She declared that the directors should be involved right from the beginning, lest the board be seen as a rubber stamp. She had a point, but unfortunately, she did not insist on voting against the proposal.

Chairman Rao raised apprehensions that the acquisition would move the company away from its core competency—IT. After all, Satyam did not have any skin in the game when it came to infrastructure. Dham chipped in, saying that since the transactions were among related parties, the company must demonstrate how the acquisition would increase shareholders' value.

Indian-American Krishna Palepu, a Harvard professor who specialized in corporate governance, spoke in favour of sticking to the knitting. He pointed to the proposed acquisitions having two complications, viz., unrelated diversification and related-party transactions. Both these issues, he felt, would be of concern to investors and analysts. Therefore, management needed to create a strong story for investors to take the bait that these transactions enhanced Satyam's long-term shareholder value.

T.R. Prasad agreed that infrastructure was a sure-shot growth story. But he suggested that the valuation of Maytas Properties be done in three parts: one, completed projects at actuals; two, work-in-progress in line with current market realizations and three, for land awaiting development, the market value notified by the state government be taken. For good measure, he added that if the final valuation was significantly higher than the sum of the above three valuations, full justification was to be provided for such a higher valuation.

Prof. Raju considered the pricing to be generous and advised a comprehensive justification for a valuation.

It was time for Rao to make his concluding observations. While agreeing with Palepu on related-party transactions, he said that the valuation outcome should be communicated to the stakeholders.

The board was told that the shareholders' approval for the acquisition was not needed. Jayaraman was quick to point out that the transaction, being price-sensitive, should be intimated to stock exchanges immediately. At that hour, stock markets both in India and the US were closed.

The time for discussion was over. It was time for a decision.

In board-managed organizations, the board is largely advisory in nature. When the principal promoter is still around, the vision is conceptualized by the management, while the board acts as a sounding body, albeit a serious-sounding one. Boards normally leave the final calls on organic or inorganic growth to the management, and unless they see serious mala fide, they trust the chief executive officer (CEO). So, in this case, despite serious reservations that they earnestly articulated, the highly decorated board bit the bullet and unanimously approved the proposals. Soon, the stock exchanges were briefed.

Alas, the independent directors' hearts had read the script right, but their heads chose the wrong route. Within the next 12 hours, their choice would sully the fair name of a star-studded board and plunge Satyam headlong into a crisis.

At the Investors' Call, all hell broke loose. Market analysts representing the investors were sceptical of any value addition through unrelated diversification and were dead against consideration being paid in cash—which effectively meant that there would be a payout rather than an offer of equity shares (also called consideration in kind or other than in cash). They were clear: the managing director was trying to sponge money off the cash-rich Satyam. In the end, none of the analysts sided with the board.

Herein lies the irony. The world thought the IT czar was using Satyam's money to feed his private fiefdom in exchange for land banks. In reality, he was doing the opposite, trying to replace Satyam's fictitious cash with Maytas's real asset! Yes, he was trying to bring order to the books.

The plan was evidently to show a partial payment to the privately owned Maytas Properties by squaring up the fictitious fixed deposits. The balance could be taken care of later. Investors and analysts had stymied Raju's plan of saving the company that he had once conceived, nurtured and taken to dizzying heights. The law of unintended consequences at work!

The furore in the international market was too much to handle, and Raju pulled back. The merger proposal was shelved.

Jayaraman spoke to the directors, and by a circular resolution, the approval given that evening was withdrawn late at night. Little did the board imagine that their resolution would be taken on record at the next board meet, where none of them would be present and when none of them would be members![7]

The independent directors' scepticism about the whole deal had been proven right. They were unhappy with the way their reputation was getting tarnished. The moment the proposal fell, one by one, they all resigned. In a letter on Christmas of 2008, senior board member Dr Srinivasan quit. On Sunday, 28 December, so did the two Indian-Americans, Dham and Palepu.

The following morning, Prof. Rao put in his papers. Less than a fortnight later, he would also step out of ISB.

Only the Rajus were left atop the burning deck along with co-directors Mynampati, Prasad and Prof. Raju. On 7 January 2009, the day of the confession, even the Rajus jumped ship. Two days later, the government dissolved what remained of the Satyam board.

◆

---

[7]Minutes of a board meeting are approved either by circulation or at the next meeting. Even if it is approved by circulation, it will be taken on record and noted in the subsequent board meeting. In this case, as none of the government-nominated directors were present in the earlier board meeting, we did not approve the minutes or resolutions passed by the earlier board but these were simply taken on record.

New Delhi
8 January 2009

Minister Prem Chand Gupta moved in to fill the leadership gap at Satyam.

MCA Secretary Anurag Goel, IAS, began making phone calls. It had not even been 24 hours since Raju's confession, but India had no time to lose. The first call was made to Kiran Karnik.

'Sir, this is Anurag Goel, Secretary, Ministry of Corporate Affairs.'

'Yes, Anurag.'

Goel came straight to the point. 'The government wants you to be part of the new board of Satyam.'

Kiran was known for his work in the broadcasting and outsourcing industries. An alumnus of the Indian Institute of Management Ahmedabad (IIM-A), the Padma Shri awardee had spent 10 years as president of NASSCOM. Given his extensive association with the industry, he was a great choice.

'When do you want me?'

'Within the next few days, Sir. We will revert.'

Then the next call went.

'Deepak Parekh here.'

'Sir, this is Anurag Goel, Secretary, Ministry of Corporate Affairs.'

'Yes, Anurag.'

'The government wants you to be part of the new board of Satyam.'

An immensely respected banker and a Padma Bhushan awardee, Deepak accepted the responsibility without a second thought.

Finally, Anurag reached C. Achuthan. A member of the Securities Appellate Tribunal in SEBI, the legal eagle was the architect of India's modern capital market jurisprudence. He too was ready to lend his expertise.

Kiran Karnik. Deepak Parekh. C. Achuthan. A trio of outstanding men: one with a deep insight into the IT industry; another, an extraordinary banker; and the third, a person who knew law like the palm of his hand. It was the proper antidote to the beleaguered Satyam, and the government could not have picked better names.

Three down, and there were a few more to go.

That afternoon, the government got in touch with another Padma Bhushan awardee. Tarun Das had been the chief mentor of the Confederation of Indian Industry (CII). He was on first-name terms with people across multiple sectors. It was too important a role for him to refuse.

Late that evening, I received a call on my handset from the MCA. Since my presidential days at the Institute of Chartered Accountants of India (ICAI), I had been closely associated with the ministry. I took the call.

At the other end was Anurag, checking my willingness to take up India's most important job at the time, viz., sitting on Satyam's board.

To me, this was a no-brainer.

My father, T.L. Narayanaswamy Chowdhry, was a freedom fighter who had been imprisoned several times by the British. The Tamil Nadu government honoured him by including his name in the Freedom Fighters' list. Thus, after a particular stage in my life, I always wanted to make my exit from active practice as a chartered accountant (CA) and serve India. When the offer came, I accepted with alacrity. Who would let go of the opportunity to serve the country? And who would miss the chance to redeem my profession, the audit profession, which was sullied by the accounting scandal at Satyam?

I had had a similar experience earlier. In 2008, the country's apex bank, the Reserve Bank of India (RBI), had nominated former IAS officer A.K.D. Jadhav, veteran banker H.N. Sinor and me as independent directors of the troubled Sahara India Financial Corporation Limited. Our mandate was to protect depositors' interests and ensure smooth repayment over five years. We completed the job in three years.

Further, my experience at the ICAI for six years, first as a council member and later as the president, would be handy. I knew Satyam was a bigger game played on a giant-sized amphitheatre and watched by many worldwide. There wasn't a chance I would let slip such an opportunity to serve the nation.

The same night, I began to follow the media coverage more closely to understand what was happening in the once storied company.

◆

On 9 January, the government moved a petition invoking sections 388B, 397, 398 and 401 to 408 of the Companies Act, 1956, before the Company Law Board (CLB). On the same day, the CLB, acting with great speed, suspended the existing board of directors and allowed the government to constitute a new board with not more than 10 persons of eminence.

The new board was asked to meet within seven days of their formation. They were to take necessary action to resurrect the company and submit periodical reports to the government on the state of its affairs.

That night, the MCA asked me to mail my profile and the names of companies in which I was a director. I sent my CV at 11.15 p.m., and 60 minutes later, in the wee hours of 10 January, I mailed the list of my directorships. I confirmed that I had neither shares nor any dealings with Satyam, which would constitute a conflict of interest.

On 11 January, the government announced that Kiran Karnik, Deepak Parekh and C. Achuthan were the new directors. It was a Sunday, but it did not matter; after all, we had weathered a national crisis.

The three of them scheduled the first board meeting for the very next day, 12 January. Everyone was eager to know the outcome of the meeting. So was I.

In the evening that day, Deepak told the media that Satyam's revival process had begun. Kiran, who chaired the day's meeting, pointed out that the board's number one priority was to restore public confidence by ensuring business continuity. For good measure, he added, 'In the past few hours that we have been here [Hi-Tech City], we have been impressed by the commitment of the officials. Many Satyamites have reached out reaffirming their commitment to the company and their desire to see Satyam reach greater heights.'[8]

There were words of assurance for the customers as well. 'The government is keen to do everything possible to quickly get the organisation on its feet and conduct business as usual.'[9]

Sitting before the television and watching the stalwarts speak, I realized it would be an opportunity of a lifetime to work with these three wise men. The thought gave me goosebumps. I was on my mark, set and waited for the word 'go' to come from the MCA in the form of official communication.

Earlier, I had told my wife, Dr Sujatha, a dental surgeon, and our two daughters, Malavika and Sahini, that the government had chosen me for a board slot in Satyam to resurrect the company. I also briefed my partners in my accounting firm, Manohar Chowdhry & Associates.

It meant I would be unavailable to them until Satyam was revived. This situation was not new to either my family or my firm. Between 5 February 2005 and 4 February 2007, I was

---

[8]Julka, Harsimran, 'Government to Appoint More Board Members Soon: Parekh', *The Economic Times*, 12 January 2009, https://bit.ly/3OObpQE. Accessed on 7 July 2022.

[9]'Deepak Parekh's Speech after Satyam Board Meeting and Excerpts from Press Meet', *Business Standard*, 20 January 2013, https://bit.ly/3SIE4sD. Accessed on 11 August 2022.

initially the vice president and later president of the ICAI. During that time, I lived in New Delhi and hardly visited my home or my office in Chennai. My family and my colleagues understood the nation's call and were very happy for me.

In the meantime, the Life Insurance Corporation of India (LIC) sought a board representation in Satyam. The Corporation, one of the most significant shareholders, had a 4.34 per cent stake.[10] With the MCA giving its nod, LIC nominated S. Balakrishna Mainak, a CA, who would one day become managing director of the insurance behemoth.

On the afternoon of 15 January, the auspicious day that marked the onset of the festival of Pongal, Anurag told me that the MCA would name three more directors, including me. I reached out to my parents at Rajakoil village near Gudiyatham, in Vellore, some 165 kilometres from Chennai, and took their blessings.

That evening, three names were announced to make a six-member board: Tarun Das, S. Balakrishna Mainak and I—and the MCA passed the necessary order.

The PMO had cleared each of the six names. The MCA still needed time to process LIC's nomination on the board, resulting in the staggered announcements.

◆

Calls started to pour in as the news of my appointment spread. The media was keen on knowing what our mandate was. 'The objective now is to protect the interests of the employees, customers and investors, and if this is achieved, everything else will fall into place,' I told them. I was seasoned enough to decline answering questions about the fraud.

Many of my fellow professionals, friends and well-wishers

---

[10] 'LIC Assessing Investment in Satyam', *The Economic Times*, 8 January 2009, https://bit.ly/3bivRL0. Accessed on 1 August 2022.

congratulated me on my appointment. They believed that the faith reposed in me by the government was not misplaced. A few suggested that it may be dangerous to be associated with a failing entity. They cared for my welfare. A botched experiment could sully my name. But I believe that challenges are given only to those who can handle them bravely.

Several CAs, who were my former students, either called, mailed or texted me to convey their best wishes. For 12 years, between 1988 and 2000, I had taught taxation to aspiring CAs. They were spread across the world and were thrilled that the government had hand-picked their guru. A few texted, 'The right man for the right job.' One told me, 'Greater congratulations will be in order when you turn the company around.' Touché.

This overwhelming response struck me. I decided I would do my best to restore Satyam's glory.

As I got ready to take the flight to Hyderabad, I reminisced about the past. I recalled how I used to wish 'best of luck for your exam' to students who either attended my classes or had read my textbook. Now it was their turn to wish me 'the best'!

When I stepped into Satyam's headquarters on the morning of 17 January 2009, I realized that I needed the 'very best', and in no small measure.

◆

Outcome of the Board Meeting

January 12, 2009

A very good evening to all of you

We have concluded the preliminary discussions of the first meeting of the Board constituted by the Central Government, today.

The top priority of the Board is to restore confidence of the customers, employees, suppliers and investors by ensuring business continuity.

An issue of this enormity will need careful consideration and extended, meaningful reviews, before it is resolved. We will, however, attempt to give you an overview. It is important to recognize though, that the Board may not be in a position to communicate the details on many issues, at this juncture. We will try and answer some of the questions that may be uppermost in all our minds, today.

The Government is going to appoint a few more Board members soon, immediately after which the full Board will decide the appointment of the Chairman.

Given the enormity of the issue and the urgent attention required, the Board will have to meet frequently for the next few months.

We are in the process of appointing an independent accounting firm within the next 48 hours to restate the financials and announce the Q3 results.

In the past few hours that we have been here, we have been impressed by the commitment of the officers that we have met. Many Satyamites have reached out reaffirming their commitment to the company and their desire to see Satyam reach greater heights. The associates are definitely of high quality and they have shown tremendous resilience and commitment, amidst all the adversity that they have been subjected to. We are told that they have united and rallied to get Satyam out of this crisis. We feel assured that they will show the same determination to deliver high quality work as per the SLAs, and help restore the glory for this organization.

We are also impressed with the marquee customers that Satyam has, which reads like the who is who of the global corporations. We like to assure Satyam's customers that our immediate priority is to ensure sustainability of services with minimal disruption. The Government is keen to do everything possible to quickly get the organization on its feet and conduct business as usual.

Working capital issues require immediate attention and we will work with the team to tide over this situation.

Thank you for joining us today. We will convene soon and update you on further developments.

PART 2

INSIDE SATYAM

3

TESTING THE WATERS

Friday, 16 January 2009

At 7 a.m., while I was waiting at the Kamaraj Domestic Airport in Chennai, an unknown number flashed on my mobile. It was the television journalist Barkha Dutt inviting me to join an NDTV debate on Satyam that night. She said that once I agreed, her office would take care of all the logistics.

I politely declined.

She insisted, suggesting that I could at least join over the phone. I did not want to discuss Satyam in public without first gaining a grip on the ground reality. If I did participate, I would only be speculative, not authentic. Realizing I was unwilling, she left it for a different day.

Soon, the boarding call came, and I made my way to India's Silicon Valley to honour a professional commitment.

That day, at 5.30 p.m, I sat in the lounge at the Kempegowda International Airport in Bengaluru, awaiting the departure call to Hyderabad. 'Beginning now,' I told myself, 'my mind and time will be exclusively devoted to Satyam.'

The splendid airport had been opened to traffic about seven months ago, on 24 May 2008. I philosophically thought, 'If India makes up its mind, it can do anything.' At that moment, I knew I, too, would make a difference to Satyam.

An hour later, I landed in the city of the Nizams.

During my years as ICAI's council member, I have seen several airports across the world, and I must say the Rajiv Gandhi International Airport is a sight to behold. Located in Shamshabad, 24 kilometres south of Hyderabad, the airport was opened on 23 March 2008. Just two months separated the Bengaluru and Hyderabad airports' birth and had given the two cities a new lease of life.

I told myself that Satyam, too, would see a new dawn, and I would do whatever it takes to make that happen.

I had my laptop in one bag and clothes for the next day's board meeting in the other. Satyam's airport representative received me and guided me to the cab. A man in a sparkling white uniform opened the rear door, and I slid into the car, wanting to catch a wink.

Soon, the car zoomed on the expressway that connects the airport with the city, and the chauffeur began to make conversation.

'How was the flight, Sir?'

'It was wonderful.'

'Congratulations on becoming a director of Satyam.'

'Thank you very much.'

Apparently, Corporate Services had briefed the chauffeur about his guest!

The drive from Shamshabad to my Hotel Taj Krishna in Banjara Hills was a 30-kilometre stretch. Unable to sleep, I sat immersed in my thoughts of the future. I was shaken out of my trance when the chauffeur began to speak again in Telugu mixed with English: 'Sir, can you put in a word to the finance team to clear dues to my travel agency?'

Ha, so Corporate Services hadn't tutored him, after all. What could I say? 'Sure, we will do our best.' I could have ignored him, but that's not in my DNA.

At the hotel, I was given a royal reception. My check-in had been done, and the duty manager, not a bellboy, escorted me up to my room. In the comfort of my room, even as I signed the papers, the manager hinted that hotel bills were outstanding and asked, 'Can you, as a director, do anything about it?'

I had the eerie feeling that he emphasized the words 'as a director'. I slowly began to get the hang of what I would be up against. But when I went to bed that night, I looked forward to the task of putting Satyam back on its track and one day on its pedestal. How and when we would do it, I didn't know. All I knew was together, we, the board, would definitely do it.

◆

Saturday, 17 January 2009

Satyam owns two massive campuses in Hyderabad. The first is in Satyam Infocity in Madhapur, which I visited for the meeting. Housed on 19.72 acres, with 1,680,000 square feet of constructed area, this campus is spectacular. A second campus, Satyam Technology Center (STC) in Bahadurpally, Ranga Reddy district, is on 118 acres, with buildings measuring 1,981,510 square feet. It is another marvel. At that time, I didn't know I would be on the board of this company for the next 12 years and still counting.

But for now, the time for being on cloud nine at being nominated to the board was over. It was time for action.

I am an early riser. It's an old habit I formed during my days as a CA teacher. After a workout in the gym, there was the small matter of signing a few papers required under the Companies Act. Satyam's company secretary Jayaraman, who would be a source of great support to us over the next many critical days, had sent these in.

At 8.30 a.m., I checked out of the hotel, as there was no need to return after the board meeting. I was told it would be an hour's drive to reach the corporate office. We reached Satyam Infocity ahead of time. Once the guard at the security check was happy with my papers, he saluted and let the vehicle pass through.

My wristwatch showed 9.20 a.m. when I walked into the corporate office.

I could instantly sense that the Satyam associates (at Satyam, employees are called associates) were tense and anxious. They knew a full board meeting was scheduled for the day to decide damage control and chalk out a road map. Instead of the carnival atmosphere that you associate with a technology company, a pall of gloom had descended on everyone. It was understandable. After all, the past 10 days had been the worst 10 days of their life. Some felt it was only a matter of time before the empire Raju had painstakingly built would collapse.

Regardless, the Satyam leadership had faith in itself and the company, and this stemmed partly from the government's proactive intervention and quick steps to replace the existing board. One thing was certain—Satyam associates felt deserted but not orphaned. The stature and standing of Kiran Karnik, Deepak Parekh, Tarun Das and C. Achuthan generated hope and optimism. Placing trust in these distinguished men had been a positive move on the government's part to calm the stakeholders' minds. I was fairly unknown in the corporate world despite being part of the RBI-nominated board of Sahara. S. Balakrishna Mainak's presence meant shareholders' voices would be heard.

As the clock chimed at 10 a.m., it was time for the second meeting of the government-nominated board. Tarun, Mainak and I joined Kiran, Deepak and Achuthan to make it the full complement of six hats.

◆

After the exchange of introductions and pleasantries, we got down to business. Jayaraman was in attendance. First, we had to decide on who would be the chairman of the company. You need a general, visible to the public, to lead a war. And Satyam's revival was nothing short of a war.

Jayaraman read out the 9 January order of the CLB. It explicitly stipulated, 'The Central Government may also designate one of them as the Chairman of the Board.'[1]

So, we decided to wait for communication from the government. Until then, we would chair by rotation. Since Kiran chaired the previous meeting held on 12 January, we elected Deepak to chair this one.

Satyam was being represented by Latham & Watkins in the US. We needed an eminent law firm in India to handle the several issues arising out of the crisis. Satyam had an in-house legal team led by General Counsel K.B. Iyappa, but it was time to look beyond, given the international ramifications. Amarchand & Mangaldas & Suresh A Shroff & Co, Advocates & Solicitors, New Delhi, were appointed as legal advisors, and the necessary resolution passed.

Shardul S. Shroff, the law firm's managing partner, and his wife, Pallavi Shroff, were called into the boardroom. The duo had done their homework. They gave an overview of the steps to be taken to protect Satyam's interests. Additionally, they emphasized the necessity to take proactive measures in the US to thwart any unforeseen issues from cropping up. We requested the Shroffs to interact with the Satyam in-house legal team, discuss with the US counsels Latham & Watkins and report on the US cases' position. We further asked them to take steps to meet the regulatory requirements for defending claims in the US and keep us updated on these matters.

---

[1]'Satyam Fraud Has Dented India Inc's Image Abroad: Govt', *The Economic Times*, 10 January 2009, https://bit.ly/3PgPVfL. Accessed on 12 July 2022.

Earlier, on 13 January, six days after Raju's sensational confession, the statutory auditors, Price Waterhouse (PW), had written to the board. They stated that the audits performed from the quarter ending on 30 June 2000 until the quarter ending on 30 September 2008, 33 in all, were based on books and records produced by the management. As Raju had disowned these, PW indicated, 'We wish to advise that the Company should promptly notify any person or entity that is known to be relying upon or is likely to rely upon our audit report that our audit opinion should no longer be relied upon.'[2] The board asked Jayaraman to place the PW communication before the legal advisor.

After this, the board took note of several things. The first was a caveat petition filed by the RoC with the High Court of Andhra Pradesh. In the legal system, any party apprehending someone approaching the court to get a stay order or injunction can file a caveat so that the court cannot pass an order without hearing the party. In this case, it meant that the court should issue notice to the Union of India's counsel and the RoC of Andhra Pradesh was to be issued before admitting any writ or any company-appeal against the 9 January order of the CLB. Second, a letter dated 12 January 2009 from the Directorate of Enforcement (ED), Hyderabad, requesting us to furnish the details required in an inquiry under the Foreign Exchange Management Act, 1999, and the Prevention of Money Laundering Act, 2002. The third was a note on the independent investigation process prepared by international counsels Latham & Watkins. And finally, we asked the secretary to present compliance matters relating to corporate laws, listing agreements and SEC, US.

It was now time to hear the business leaders of the company. T.R. Anand, Ravi Bommakanti, Sriram Papani and

---

[2]'PW: Don't Rely on Our Opinion on Satyam', *The Telegraph Online*, 15 January 2009, https://bit.ly/3SdVSf7. Accessed on 1 August 2022.

Dr Keshab Panda briefed us about the situation on the customer front. They requested the board to talk to customers and reassure them of the company's status. We agreed.

The finance team consisting of V. Ramesh Kumar, V. Venkatakumar Raju and G. Subramanian presented Satyam's precarious situation. It looked like we had to infuse at least ₹500 crore for the associates' pay cheque.

Non-payment of statutory dues resulting in freezing Satyam's bank account by the Income Tax Department, issuing notices by other agencies and vendors threatening to pull out were highlighted. Banks were pressuring them to settle their dues. And while the team had deposited customer collections into Satyam's bank account, the banks were quietly appropriating it against the money due to them. Certainly unfair, but true nevertheless. The normal practice is that when a bank receives money in its customer's account, it is the customer who decides how to use that money. Here, as soon as money landed in the account, the bank appropriated or used it to settle dues to themselves. Next, the board picked the legal advisors'—Amarchand & Mangaldas—brains on the critical question of whether the new directors would be hauled up for legal infractions of the past. In pursuance of the CLB order, the Government of India, through the MCA, had appointed us as directors. The CLB is a quasi-judicial body that carries out some of the courts' functions in company law matters, and we were officers of the government. The legal advisors felt it was essential to obtain immunity for the new board's actions by moving the CLB. We promptly gave the go-ahead to file the necessary documents.

◆

Soon, it was time for lunch as the clock in the boardroom showed 1.30 p.m. I wondered at how quickly the clock hands had moved.

We were ushered to a well-furbished dining hall meant for directors, executives and invitees. A tall pile of menus, neatly stacked, greeted us, covering a wide range of cuisines. There was a choice between vegetarian and non-vegetarian. The chef and caterers, in impressive uniform, served hot Indian breads, such as roti, phulka and naan.

Those who built this empire, brick-by-brick, were in jail, and by a queer turn of events, a stranger like me, unconnected with the company, was having lunch here. With these thoughts plaguing my mind, I suddenly lost my appetite and taste for the food served.

During the lunch break, I got a glimpse of the corporate office and its infrastructure, including the former chairman and former managing director's chambers. The architectural design was a marvel. The two adjacent buildings, A Wing and B Wing, were connected by a bridge-like structure about 200 feet long and 60 feet wide. It appeared as though hanging in the air on the fifth floor. It accommodated these two cabins and the respective secretariat offices. A walk-through passage connecting the two buildings with a pathway garden of flower plants, shrubs and pebbles was a treat to the eyes.

The Rajus never compromised on quality for the sake of trimming the budget. The campus's grandeur, the magnificent design of its buildings and its state-of-the-art interiors were admirable. It was difficult to digest that the men who had such incredible passion for building world-class infrastructure succumbed, for whatever reason, to short-changing the company they founded. It was hard to believe that Satyam, once the cynosure of all eyes, was now in the spotlight for all the wrong reasons.

Over lunch, the board informally continued the conversation with both Shardul and Pallavi Shroff. We agreed that we needed to engage a firm for carrying out a proper forensic investigation and restatement of financial statements from 2001–02 onwards.

A forensic audit is a process of examining financial records to unearth fraud evidence admissible in a court of law. We felt we must engage a multinational accounting firm because of Satyam's global presence and it being listed on the NYSE. Among the 'Big Four' firms, while PW was ruled out as action was triggered against them by the investigating agencies for the Satyam fraud and Ernst & Young was perceived as associated with Maytas, the choice narrowed down to KPMG and Deloitte.

Considering that six years of transactions were to be covered and the urgency demanded by the situation, the legal advisors felt it would be appropriate to jointly engage KPMG and Deloitte. It made a lot of sense.

SATYAM VERTICALS

Satyam's customers were segregated based on different regions, such as North America and South America (called Americas) under Ram Mynampati (until he resigned in June 2009), Europe under Dr Keshab Panda and the Rest of the World predominantly comprising Asia Pacific, the Middle East and Africa under Virender Aggarwal.

In terms of verticals, Ram led Commercial and Healthcare Businesses and T.R. Anand was in charge of Telecom, Tech Infrastructure, Media and Entertainment, and Semiconductors. Dr Panda was responsible for Energy and Utilities and D. Subbu headed the Manufacturing and Automotive Group.

There were several verticals managed by other leaders. To name a few important ones—SAP and Testing by Manish Mehta, Enterprise Application by Sriram Papani, Business Intelligence by Kiran Cavale, Consulting and Enterprise Solutions by Joseph Lagioia and Application Development, Maintenance and Support (ADMS) by Ravi Bommakanti.

Other support services functions had their own bosses: Jayaraman for Secretarial and Corporate Services, Vijay Prasad for Soft Infrastructure Group, T. Hari for Marketing and Communications, S.V. Krishnan for Human Resources, V. Murali for Commercial, A.S. Murthy for Global Delivery, Nick Sharma for Networking and Systems and Rajan Nagarajan for Solutions.

During the revival phase, most of these leaders did a phenomenal job of staying connected to key customers and associates.

4

MITIGATION MEASURES

Post-lunch, when the members were settling down in the boardroom to carry on with the agenda, I made a suggestion. 'As we are doing it for the country, we should not take any compensation for this assignment regardless of the time it takes us to revive Satyam.'

Tarun smiled, and I still recall his words, 'Good idea, Manoharan. In fact, we should not even take any sitting fee for attending board meetings.'

Chairman Parekh had the final say, 'We are doing this pro bono.' His voice boomed across the boardroom, and we all agreed. Later, in my various public talks across the world, whenever I clarified the board worked without taking a rupee, the response was rapturous.

After that, we discussed with the top management of Satyam BPO Limited. This is a wholly owned subsidiary, and to our dismay, we found their net worth had eroded. It meant their accumulated losses were greater than equity capital. We also learnt that board positions of this company had to be filled. The company secretary agreed to bring this up at the board meeting, fixed for 22 and 23 January.

Next, we had a few unscheduled visitors. Of course, they called before dropping in. They were representatives of the state Crime Branch-Criminal Investigation Department (CB-CID). Afterwards, officials from the Serious Fraud Investigation Office (SFIO) paid a courtesy visit and spent 15 minutes with us.

Meanwhile, the board constituted the audit committee comprising Achuthan, Mainak and me. I was nominated as chairman and was asked to look into the finance and internal audit aspects.

Among the first decisions the audit committee took was to recommend to the board the need to appoint an accounting firm to carry out an internal audit. In large corporates, these auditors perform process audits and test checks to verify if controls and procedures are in place. Satyam had an in-house team led by V.S.P. Gupta. On analysing the scope of work, we noticed that transactions audit was omitted. Transactions audit refers to the verification of day-to-day transactions on a sample basis. Had this been done, it is possible that the auditors could have found the fictitious nature of some of the bills. We felt that in the prevailing situation, we needed a detailed transactions audit. We wanted a firm outside Hyderabad and zeroed in on the Chennai-based Brahmayya & Co. I spoke with P.S. Kumar, senior partner of the firm, regarding the terms and conditions, which the board subsequently approved.

◆

The finance team was back in the afternoon, explaining the precarious financial position of Satyam.

As of December 2008, back-of-the-envelope calculations placed dues to suppliers and service providers at ₹2,000 crore, monthly salary bill at ₹500 crore and other administrative expenses at ₹100 crore. Provident fund (PF) and tax deducted at source (TDS) needed to be remitted for December—a statutory default could have severe legal ramifications. Could salary commitments be honoured on time in these conditions? the leadership team wondered.

Well, debtors owed Satyam ₹1,700 crore, but how much of it was genuine was pure conjecture. Worse still, even genuine customers were hesitating to make payments. They had their reservations. In case payments were made and Satyam opted out of its service commitment, they felt that alternative service providers would have to be engaged. That would escalate the project cost. Instead, if they held back payments to Satyam, they could migrate to a competitor and complete the project without cost overruns.

There were further shocks on the customer front. A few customers wanted to terminate the agreement as they did not want to be associated with a tainted company. We understood their stand, but at the same time, we were determined to arrest this trend by revamping the sullied image of Satyam.

Citibank and BNP Paribas—Satyam's bankers —wanted the working capital and term loan arrangements to be squared immediately and the bank guarantee closed. Till then, Satyam had been a premium customer at whose doorstep bankers would wait for hours on end. Suddenly, it had become a persona non grata. With Citi and BNP put together, Satyam and Satyam BPO had an overall ₹750 crore exposure. This included fund-based, non-fund-based and foreign exchange hedging facilities.[1]

During this time, the foreign banks transferred the balances in every Satyam account abroad to India to secure for them as much as possible. As overseas salary accounts in all the countries were with Citibank, BNP Paribas or HSBC, Satyam defaulted on its obligations in some of those jurisdictions.

We spoke to Jose K. Joseph, Commercial Banking-Risk, Citibank. (Over time, he would rise to become managing director and chief credit officer for Citibank North America.) We told him, 'Do treat Satyam as a going concern, extend us full support in the national interest and be part of the

---

[1] Fund-based limits are the ones where the bank lends money to the client. Non-fund-based limits do not involve moneylending; for example, bank guarantee. Foreign exchange hedging refers to taking derivative positions like forward contract, which mitigate the risk of exchange rate fluctuations.

solution provider.' We suggested the bank return the money appropriated towards packing credit. Also called pre-shipment credit, packing credit is a loan granted to an exporter for financing the purchase, processing, manufacturing or packing of goods prior to shipment. These respectively relate to raw material, work in progress and finished goods. We reiterated to Citi that Satyam's strength lay in its negligible debts, large receivables and healthy fixed assets. We even agreed to provide a second charge on receivables or fixed assets up to 200 per cent of outstanding fund-based limits. In exchange, we wanted the bank to not make changes to the non-fund-based limits. A person who has first charge has the first right over an asset if there is a default. A person with a second charge has a second and subsequent right over the asset. This implies that the person having second charge can recover any amount only if there is surplus beyond the amount due to the person having the first charge. Citi indicated its inability to reverse appropriations already made but assured us of being considerate in the future. They wanted to discuss the issue of continuing the facilities with a board representative.

The board also met BNP Paribas's Frédéric Amoudru, chief executive and country manager, and Sandeep Mehrotra, head of Corporate Credit. We asked them to stay with the company and make the collection amounts available without appropriation towards their dues. Amoudru promised to look into it.

Around this time, we learnt that the Income Tax Department completed a few assessments and raised a demand of ₹54 crore. The tax officers gave us 10 days for payment, while the law allowed up to 30 days. On the eleventh day, the department wrote to all our bankers and froze our accounts, worrying about the non-payment of dues. Obviously, the assessing officer felt it detrimental to allow the entire 30 days for payment. So, we met them in our boardroom and reached an agreement. We suggested the department accept ₹50 lakh per month commencing 20 March 2009. We promised that if the appeal went against the company, Satyam would pay the remaining amount. Based on this, the deputy commissioner of income tax, Murali Mohan, lifted the attachment.

While the central government appointed the board to resurrect Satyam, other arms of the same government fought to take parts of Satyam's assets to meet debt dues to them. In some recess of my mind, I could feel the irony.

Even as our board meeting was in session, there were calls from customers such as Nestlé, Walmart, Caterpillar, National Australia Bank and Nissan. We distributed these calls amongst ourselves, and with the members of the top management by our side, we responded to queries. We reassured our customers that Satyam would continue to work on projects and deliver on time without compromising on quality.

As the meeting progressed, three priorities became clear to the board. Our first job was to restore fiscal sanity. Second, we needed to ensure customers were assured of continuity and smooth delivery of services. Finally, we needed to engage with associates and motivate them to join hands with us in our endeavour to revive Satyam.

We agreed one of us would camp in Hyderabad, oversee the execution of the board's decisions and be accessible to customers worldwide. This would ensure the business's day-to-day administration was attended to. I volunteered to remain full time for Satyam as I was mentally prepared for it. During my presidential years at ICAI, I had relocated to Delhi for two whole years. So, staying away from home or the office wasn't anything new for me. Both Achuthan and Mainak offered to be available at the headquarters in turns and made themselves available periodically in rotation.

Indeed, my contribution may not have been significant at the macro level compared to the legends on the board, but I am delighted to have devoted my entire time and effort to

Satyam's revival by managing things at the micro level until the new owners came along.

◆

The legal advisors wanted me to join a discussion with KPMG and Deloitte on the sidelines of the board meeting. This was to discuss the restatement of accounts. So, I stepped into the adjoining room. There, I met Udayan Sen, CEO, Deloitte India. I also met Russell Parera, CEO, KPMG India, and his colleague Deepankar Sanwalka, head of Forensic Services.

We discussed the scope of work with the two firms and the need to restate accounts at the earliest. I told the two firms' representatives that this engagement was only about two things: one, identifying fraudulent accounting transactions; and two, assisting Satyam in preparing restated financials. Towards this, I wanted them to allocate adequate talent and chalk out an action plan. The firms must write to banks and customers for confirmation of balances and restructure the customer ledger accounts. I also suggested identifying every related-party transaction and analysing both current assets and liabilities. They had to compare and reconcile, using data analytics, the internally generated data with what was obtained externally from customers, vendors, banks and other agencies. The team should collate, secure and analyse electronic data, including emails, to get information to decipher the fraud.

I made it clear we were running out of time, and the assignment ought to be on the fast track. For clarity, I added this assignment was of national importance triggered by the government's initiative to revive the company and protect its stakeholders. We were looking to being charged a discounted price.

They understood and appreciated these aspects. On their part, they explained that there was significant complexity because the company's verticals operated in silos, there were no reconciliations and the volume of operations was enormous. They felt they might have to perform extensive procedures to obtain corroborative evidence. The work had to be as per the standard acceptable to the US regulator SEC, SEBI and other regulatory bodies. The disclaimer by PW of opinions issued had increased the scope of work in restating financial statements.

I heard them out and could understand their point of view.

Both KPMG and Deloitte promised to form a team comprising four partners responsible for project leadership and direction, 16 partners/directors for leading various work streams, 19 managers and 34 staff, with 90 per cent of them postgraduate equivalent. The team was tilted towards senior-level personnel in contrast to a regular audit engagement, given the seriousness of the assignment. Of course, the team's size and composition were open to change as the engagement progressed.

The firms could not provide an exact time frame, given the alleged fraud's nature and limited knowledge of how it was perpetrated. On the cost factor, they assured me they would be reasonable in their fee quote. I left them to discuss with our legal advisors and rejoined the board meeting.

As the meeting neared completion, there were calls from the media. Deepak suggested we do a press release now and meet the media only after we achieved a milestone. It made a lot of sense.

In the press release, we said we were on the lookout for a full-time CEO and a full-time CFO. We said our business leaders were continuing their job seamlessly. The board clarified it was in touch with customers, deliveries had not been affected and employees continue to perform high-quality work. We also said we talked with banks and financial institutions, collections from customers had begun and employees would be paid on time.

As our meeting neared the end, we learnt some journalists were waiting for us at the main gate. So, in batches, we left through the rear entrance to reach the airport. It surprised me the media didn't guess this. Of course, some were waiting at the airport, and when they tried to talk to us, we smiled, ducked and boarded our flight. Maybe the paparazzi culture hadn't yet begun in India in January 2009!

So, it was late that night on 17 January that I returned to Chennai to pack my bags and relocate to Hyderabad: lock, stock and barrel.

♦

The following morning, a Sunday, I was at the breakfast table in my house, sipping traditional filter coffee. A journalist from Delhi called. During my tenure as ICAI president, I addressed the press once in a fortnight between 12 and 1.30 p.m. to update them on the progressive measures taken by the council. This would be followed by lunch. It was here that I made friends with the media. This was to ensure they could file their story in time for the next morning's paper.

The caller was K.R. Srivats of *The Hindu BusinessLine* from New Delhi. He wanted to know what was cooking! We spoke for a while, and he finally took the liberty of asking point-blank, 'Sir, knowing the grave situation in which Satyam is placed, don't you think it is next to impossible to turn it around? Besides, this being an interim arrangement by the government, your board position is temporary, and therefore what can you do?'

With all the humility at my command, I said, 'Srivats, we are all temporary in this world, but we can build permanent institutions. We can resurrect companies that can have perpetual succession. We can imbibe values that last for generations to follow and practise principles that would be eternal. Maybe we are mortals, but these are not.'

He couldn't agree with me more.

♦

That evening, the Satyam Leadership Council gave us a hint of urgency, in case we weren't clear about the need for speed!

Forty-five men representing each constituent group in the company wrote to the board, pouring their heart out in a letter that had anguish written all over it. Everyone, be it the head of customer-facing units, or technology and consulting practice, or geographical locations and support groups, was party to the letter. It was a single email sent out by the leadership team to Jayaraman. The council saw him as the bridge between the leadership and the board. Given its urgency, Jayaraman forwarded it to us immediately at 7.31 p.m.

Titled 'SOS', the letter was a passionate request for help to lift Satyam from the morass. They said the government's action and board members' iconic stature had helped retain most marquee customers for the last two weeks. But they feared customers had contingency plans and that Satyam had already lost 20 per cent of its existing business with the exit of one of its longest-standing customers. This would be a business loss of over $100 million annually and impact 1,000 associates. Another $100 million could be gone if two other large customers who were talking about transition walked the talk.

The leadership team also gave suggestions. They felt two actions could temporarily salvage the situation if the message went out latest by Monday, 19 January. Yes, they were giving the board 24 hours' time to make decisions. The first was a public commitment that salaries would be honoured and an assurance that Satyam had long-term viability. Second, the appointment of a CEO would show that the company was in control of things. Beyond the 19th, it would be too late, they reasoned.

Besides, they requested for infusion of funds as a bridge loan from the government. They concluded, saying, 'Let us somehow SAVE SATYAM. We want to retain India's pride.'

It was not that we did not know how anguished they were, but the letter reinforced our belief, and the tone and tenor of the appeal only strengthened our resolve to find an early solution.

The next day, I was back in Hyderabad to begin my work with renewed enthusiasm.

But, before taking you through the turn of events inside Satyam, let me highlight the two conflicting faces of B. Ramalinga Raju.

◆

LEADERS WRITE TO THE BOARD

To : The Respected Board Members

SOS: A Passionate Appeal

Dear Sirs

We are writing this on behalf of the Leadership Council – a group of about 45 leaders representing every key constituent group in the company. (Customer facing units, technology & consulting practices, geographical representation and support units).

This note is a passionate appeal – brought upon us by the tragic developments and the consequent experiences in the field. Kindly do bear with us, if we sound anguished and urgent. We want to highlight our plight.

Firstly, please accept our sincere and heartfelt appreciation to each one of you for taking up this daunting responsibility at such short notice – a responsibility that has been thrust upon you in these trying circumstances. Every single Satyamite (and their extended families) will forever be grateful to you, as you steer us through this calamity.

The Government's timely action, your iconic stature and our hard-earned customer relationships have helped us to hold on to most of our marquee customers, for the last two weeks.

We are noticing that increasingly, the customers are highlighting that they have a choice. They have made their contingency plans or are in the process of communicating one.

In the last one week :

- We have lost almost 20% of the existing business.

    - One of our biggest and longest standing Insurance customer has asked us to transition the work to other vendors. This will be a business loss in excess of USD 100 Mn. annually and will impact about 1000 associates – 400 of them onsite.

    - We have two very large customers – a beverage major and a Insurance major – who are talking to us about transition right now. This will total another USD 100 mn. or more

- We have lost almost ALL our recent wins. These are deals in the USD 50 Mn and above range. The Telecome major's Billion dollar deal looks seriously jeopardized as of now. We are having serious challenges salvaging these.

MITIGATION MEASURES

<u>A quick and definitive action can help save 50% of the business that may otherwise be lost, next week.</u>

The only thing that can help obtain temporary relief are two direct and definitive statements, by Monday (19th Jan 2009) :

1. **We have to make a firm statement on employee salaries & welfare and the long term viability of Satyam.**
2. **We have to show that the organization has one leader for now – even if it is for the interim, who is in control of things. It can be anyone that the Board may choose from within.**

Rapid Revenue shrinkage at the current cost base will call for crucial and difficult actions later and spiral us downwards, even faster. We are afraid that any help after Monday the 19th Jan 2009, may be seen as having come too late. Customers may and in all probability, will not wait !

Funding, based on receivables as collateral, may take time. Could we help influence the government for a bridge loan in the meantime? We assure you that we will fight back to win again.

WE DO NOT NEED TAXPAYERS' MONEY.

<u>Please let our customers and Associates know something concrete by Monday evening India time.</u>

Let us somehow SAVE SATYAM. We want to retain India's pride - we are definitely working for the India story.

Warm Regards

Leadership Team at Satyam.

PART 3

JANUS-FACED

5
'EDWARD HYDE' AT SATYAM

Ramalinga Raju made some stunning confessions in his email to the Satyam board, SEBI and stock exchanges. It marked out the technology major's financials as almost fictitious.

The audited financial statement of any company is the Holy Grail for shareholders. This is where management speaks the truth, the whole truth and nothing but the truth. In this report, managers outline what a company owns, what it owes, how its performance has been and what is the road ahead. Remember, these men are agents for shareholders who chipped in with money. Therefore, the conversation between the agent and shareholder is to be with candour. An external party, namely a statutory auditor, certifies whether the management is speaking the truth.

Raju was now telling the world that Satyam's financial statements were anything but genuine. Assets such as cash and bank balance, debtors and accrued interest were incorrect, he said. So were outside liabilities.

By far, cash and bank balances are the most difficult assets to fudge and the easiest to verify. To play with them requires enormous guts. But, not at Satyam! Raju said that against ₹5,361 crore shown in books, ₹5,040 crore was nonexistent.[1] Yes, 94 per cent of the money was missing, and it was like staring at a hole in a bank's strongroom. If you take the average exchange

---

[1]Figures stated in Raju's letter to the board of directors dated 7 January 2009.

rate of the year 2008–09 as ₹45.99 per dollar, this ₹5,040 crore translates into a little more than a billion dollars. No one in history had stashed away so much cash under a haystack.

Raju masterfully did it because no such money existed in the first place!

As investigations would unearth, the fudged numbers were fabricated to originate from a single bank branch in New York and five branches of various banks across India. Did the auditors seek verification from the bank about the existence of the fixed deposits? It appears so, as investigating agencies found confirmations in forged letterheads of the bank.[2] This apart, according to submissions before SEBI, the auditors relied on physical verification of fixed deposit receipts in the custody of Satyam. The banks denied giving out such receipts.[3]

The disappearance of cash was the most startling part. The others pale in comparison. Debtors represent money receivable from people for whom you have done work. The confession revealed that of the ₹2,651 crore, a good 18.5 per cent viz., ₹490 crore was fictitious. These debtors hadn't turned bad; they were not there in the first place because Satyam had not done any work for them!

Did the auditors seek confirmation of balance from debtors, and if they did, was the response forged? According to their submission before SEBI, the auditors carried out alternative procedures like verifying sales documents, subsequent realization from these debtors, etc., as confirmation of balances received from overseas debtors was uniformly negligible.[4]

---

[2]'Auditors in on Satyam Fraud: CBI', *Mint*, 7 December 2009, https://bit.ly/3yyzx2Z. Accessed on 13 July 2022.
[3]'Forged FD Receipts May Have Misled Auditor', *Business Standard*, 29 January 2013, https://bit.ly/3P3ghBK. Accessed on 13 July 2022.
[4]For the full case report, see 'Order in Respect of M/S Price Waterhouse, Bangalore', SEBI, *Casemine*, https://bit.ly/3vrTM1C. Accessed on 1 August 2022.

Raju wasn't done. He came to 'accrued interest'. The technical meaning of this term is 'interest earned but not fallen due'. Let us suppose your yearly interest of ₹25,000 on a deposit is payable by the end of March. So, on 30 September, a sum of ₹12,500 has accrued for the first half-year but not fallen due. Raju confessed that ₹376 crore of such accrued interest was false. Clearly, these were on the fake deposits! Fake interest on the phony deposit.

And finally, why disturb just the assets? What about liabilities?

In his confession letter, Raju wrote that Satyam's balance sheet as of 30 September 2008 did not carry a liability of ₹1,230 crore, which were funds ostensibly arranged by him. This meant that, if what he was saying was true, money was put into the company from private sources (37 firms) to solve its liquidity crisis. Soon, Satyam received letters from 37 of Raju's group companies seeking repayment. As there was no evidence, including authorization from the board for taking loans, Satyam declined acknowledgement and refused payment.

If you add up all the amounts mentioned in the confession letter, viz. the ₹5,040 crore, the ₹490 crore and the ₹376 crore, it translates to ₹5,906 crore on the assets side. These were matched by inflated profits of ₹5,906 crore on the liabilities side, lying under reserves! The assets were bogus to that extent, and so were the reserves.

The earnings statement of the September 2008 quarter was a holy mess. The revenue recorded was ₹2,700 crore against ₹2,112 crore, leading to an overstatement of ₹588 crore. That's about 28 per cent! The quarter's profit was reported as ₹649 crore when, in reality, it was ₹61 crore! So, the 24 per cent margin shown was, in fact, less than 3 per cent.[5]

Inflated billing, nonexistent cash and bank balance,

---

[5] As stated in Raju's letter to the board of directors dated 7 January 2009.

overstated debtors and discrepancy in the operating margin leading to fictitious reserves—Satyam had tried everything. This, which seems to have been practised for many years, had turned into a Frankenstein's monster.

So, why did it all happen, and how did it start?

◆

Perhaps it began in the aftermath of 2000. The software industry had just then cracked the Y2K code, and Satyam was a part of the global race to set the bug right. Raju wanted to keep up with the Joneses. One possibility is that maybe he wanted to be in the company of, and spoken in the same breath as, the technology industry's A-listers: Azim Premji, Narayana Murthy, Shiv Nadar and S. Ramadorai.

A second possibility is Raju ran the business very ethically from June 1987, when he incorporated Satyam, for about a decade. Subsequently, both revenue and profit dipped. Despite his best efforts to push delivery and billing, there was a gap between plan and performance. It was bound to impact the company's rating in the market and lead to a sharp fall in stock price. Possibly, someone planted this idea to the chairman to bridge the gap with fictitious numbers. Unfortunately, Raju bit the fish bait.

Let me divert a bit here. When an unfair practice is first suggested, the mind resists. But when you are told this is temporary and can be made right the next quarter, the mind wavers. It is when the moral fibre is tested. With apologies to Hamlet, it is a 'to say "yes" or not to say "yes"' dilemma. One has to ask oneself if it matters if you are fourth or fortieth in the pecking order. Do the means not justify the ends? Should you not sleep well at night?

But once you succumb to the urge to fake, you slip into quicksand. The next quarter, you tell yourself we can live the imaginary numbers just for this one year and clean up next season. Alas, it doesn't work that way. What begins as an exception becomes the rule and soon a part of you. And when even the best of audit firms don't spot the issues, you get tempted to repeat. So, the numbers keep swelling each year and ultimately snowball into a monster. Eventually, it becomes difficult to kill this tendency without shaking the painstakingly built empire.

I believe this version of 'an inherently decent man who slipped on the righteous path' when I read Raju's giveaway line in his confession, 'It was like riding a tiger, not knowing how to get off without being eaten.'

Thanks to his confession, we do know Raju had been priming profits for years. Usually, some businesses conceal profits and reduce taxes. Raju did it the other way, perhaps because the bulk of his income was from exports, and in the India of those days, export profits were tax-free.

◆

Let's quickly review a few basics of the scam.

Raju needed artificial billing to show Satyam was in the premium league. These fictitious invoices lead to ghost debtors. Such debtors cannot stay outstanding for long, so they have to be shown as collected. This is because a debtor lying beyond reasonable period is bound to create suspicions about its bona fides. In an audit, outstanding beyond six months are scrutinized. For that, bank statements were fabricated to falsely reflect a flow of money from non-executed work.

Next, what was pictured as collected had to be invested. After all, any smart individual would ask why so much money was in the current account earning nothing. So, these cash balances were converted into bogus fixed deposits backed by fake receipts. And these deposits were shown as periodically renewed! Interest income on the fictitious bank deposits was also disclosed in the income-tax return.

Let's now figure out what might have triggered the confession. There are a few theories to be considered.

When faking invoices became regular, Satyam needed to show it had the bandwidth to achieve this turnover. Satyam had 'bench' strength, namely, a workforce awaiting work, which was higher than its peers. This came in handy to support fictitious billing. Yes, while the invoices were ghosts, the operational costs were actual, and it was no wonder the operating margin nosedived.

At that time, the global financial crisis arrived unannounced. Satyam had cash flow issues and needed to raise money. But it would be a red flag since the balance sheet showed a lot of money in the bank. The high cash and bank balance should have raised the suspicion of any one of several people: the board, the auditors, the analysts or any of the many investors. Internally, some vertical heads had pointed to their turnover reflected in the audited statements being greater than what they had achieved. They were facilely told that the sale of a few software licences had been booked in their vertical. A lot of water had flown under the bridge during the second and third quarters of 2008. Things were getting out of control, and with operating losses looming large, it was time to clean up. The Rajus had pledged their shares for borrowings at a time when their holding stood at 8 per cent.

As the share prices began descending in the wake of the global financial crisis (from ₹533 in May 2008 to ₹251 in December that year),[6] the lenders applied pressure for additional securities. With no extra security forthcoming, they encashed the shares even as it hurtled down to ₹114 by the year end.

Furthermore, since promoters had a tiny percentage of equity, the threat of takeover by a third party was stark. Raju

---

[6]'Satyam Computer Services Ltd (SATY)', *Investing.com*, https://bit.ly/3PQ1afg. Accessed on 1 August 2022.

indicated much the same in his confession. 'As the promoters held a small percentage of equity, the concern was that poor performance would result in a takeover, thereby exposing the gap.' This was when Raju probably started to weigh the pros and cons of coming clean.

If outside agencies called out the fraud, the consequences could be devastating. America's SEC would instantly step in as Satyam was listed on Nasdaq. The Sultan of Software would be deported to the US for trial, and if found guilty, taken away for long. Remember Jeffrey Skilling, the former CEO of Enron, was sentenced to 24 years and four months in prison? If that happened, his entire property would have been confiscated to pay penalties and settle class-action suits. His best protection lay in coming clean on his own, trigger action from domestic law enforcement agencies and take shelter in the safe havens of Indian jurisdiction.

Another dimension is that if external agencies spotted the fraud, Raju would have to cool his heels behind bars and, worse still, Satyam might disintegrate. But if he confessed, resigned and proposed a revival plan without him, the company might survive. His letter talks about such a programme. It's another matter that the government, not he, masterminded the bounce back, as many believe. A Raju-acolyte later gushingly told me, 'The boss had put himself on the chopping block to let Satyam stay afloat.' It is possible these factors cumulatively culminated in the confession letter.

Ramalinga Raju may have been in his Mr Edward Hyde role in Robert Louis Stevenson's novella, *The Strange Case of Dr Jekyll and Mr Hyde*. There is also a very distinct Dr Henry Jekyll in him.

♦

B. Ramalinga Raju's Letter Dated 7 January 2009

To the Board of Directors
Satyam Computer Services Ltd.

From B. Ramalinga Raju
Chairman, Satyam Computer Services Ltd.   January 7, 2009

Dear Board Members,

It is with deep regret, and tremendous burden that I am carrying on my conscience, that I would like to bring the following facts to your notice:

1. The Balance Sheet carries as of September 30, 2008
    a. Inflated (non-existent) cash and bank balances of Rs.5,040 crore (as against Rs. 5361 crore reflected in the books)
    b. An accrued interest of Rs. 376 crore which is non-existent
    c. An understated liability of Rs. 1,230 crore on account of funds arranged by me
    d. An over stated debtors position of Rs. 490 crore (as against Rs. 2651 reflected in the books)

2. For the September quarter (Q2) we reported a revenue of Rs.2,700 crore and an operating margin of Rs. 649 crore (24% Of revenues) as against the actual revenues of Rs. 2,112 crore and an actual operating margin of Rs. 61 Crore (3% of revenues). This

has resulted in artificial cash and bank balances going up by Rs. 588 crore in Q2 alone.

The gap in the Balance Sheet has arisen purely on account of inflated profits over a period of last several years (limited only to Satyam standalone, books of subsidiaries reflecting true performance). What started as a marginal gap between actual operating profit and the one reflected in the books of accounts continued to grow over the years. It has attained unmanageable proportions as the size of company operations grew significantly (annualized revenue run rate of Rs. 11,276 crore in the September quarter, 2008 and official reserves of Rs. 8,392 crore). The differential in the real profits and the one reflected in the books was further accentuated by the fact that the company had to carry additional resources and assets to justify higher level of operations —thereby significantly increasing the costs.

Every attempt made to eliminate the gap failed. As the promoters held a small percentage of equity, the concern was that poor performance would result in a take-over, thereby exposing the gap. It was like riding a tiger, not knowing how to get off without being eaten.

The aborted Maytas acquisition deal was the last attempt to fill the fictitious assets with real ones. Maytas' investors were convinced that this is a good divestment opportunity and a strategic fit. Once Satyam's problem was solved, it was hoped that Maytas' payments can be delayed. But that was not to be. What followed in the last several days is common knowledge.

I would like the Board to know:

1. That neither myself, nor the Managing Director (including our spouses) sold any shares in the last eight years – excepting for a small proportion declared and sold for philanthropic purposes.

2. That in the last two years a net amount of Rs. 1,230 crore was arranged to Satyam (not reflected in the books of Satyam) to keep the operations going by resorting to pledging all the promoter shares and raising funds from known sources by giving all kinds of assurances (Statement enclosed, only to the members of the board). Significant dividend payments, acquisitions, capital expenditure to provide for growth did not help matters. Every attempt was made to keep the wheel moving and to ensure prompt payment of salaries to the associates. The last straw was the selling of most of the pledged share by the lenders on account of margin triggers.

3. That neither me, nor the Managing Director took even one rupee/dollar from the company and have not benefitted in financial terms on account of the inflated results.

4. None of the board members, past or present, had any knowledge of the situation in which the company is placed. Even business leaders and senior executives in the company, such as, Ram Mynampati, Subu D, T.R. Anand, Keshab Panda, Virender Agarwal, A.S. Murthy, Hari T, SV Krishnan, Vijay Prasad, Manish Mehta, Murali V, Sriram Papani, Kiran Kavale, Joe Lagioia, Ravindra Penumetsa, Jayaraman and Prabhakar Gupta are unaware of the real situation as against the books of accounts. None of my or Managing Director's immediate or extended family members has any idea about these issues.

Having put these facts before you, I leave it to the wisdom of the board to take the matters forward. However, I am also taking the liberty to recommend the following steps:

1. A Task Force has been formed in the last few days to address the situation arising out of the failed Maytas acquisition attempt. This consists of some of the most accomplished leaders of Satyam: Subu D, T.R. Anand, Keshab Panda and Virender Agarwal , representing business functions, and A.S. Murthy, Hari T and Murali V representing support functions. I suggest that Ram Mynampati be made the Chairman of this Task Force to immediately address some of the operational matters on hand. Ram can also act as an interim CEO reporting to the board.

2. Merrill Lynch can be entrusted with the task of quickly exploring some Merger opportunities.

3. You may have a 'restatement of accounts' prepared by the auditors in light of the facts that I have placed before you.

I have promoted and have been associated with Satyam for well over twenty years now. I have seen it grow from few people to 53,000 people, with 185 Fortune 500 companies as customers and operations in 66 countries. Satyam has established an excellent leadership and competency base at all levels. I sincerely apologize to all Satyamites and stakeholders, who have made Satyam a special organization, for the current situation. I am confident they will stand by the company in this hour of crisis.

In light of the above, I fervently appeal to the board to hold together to take some important steps. Mr. T.R. Prasad is well placed to mobilize support from the government at this crucial time. With the hope that members of the Task Force and the financial advisor, Merrill Lynch (now Bank of America) will stand by the company at this crucial hour, I am marking copies of this statement to them as well.

Under the circumstances, I am tendering my resignation as the chairman of Satyam and shall continue in this position only till such time the current board is expanded. My continuance is just to ensure enhancement of the board over the next several days or as early as possible.

I am now prepared to subject myself to the laws of the land and face consequences thereof.

(B. Ramalinga Raju)

Copies marked to:
1. Chairman SEBI
2. Stock Exchanges

6
DR HENRY JEKYLL TO THE WORLD

Ramalinga Raju will forever be remembered for his role as a social entrepreneur. It endeared him to the rich and famous as also the poor and marginalized sections of society.

The boy from a remote village, Garagaparru, in West Godavari, was a folk hero. He had a streak of social benevolence that transformed the lives of several young men in rural Andhra. In 2001, at the age of 47, he established the Byrraju Foundation in his father's memory. The foundation took care of all the villages in Bhimavaram, about 400 kilometres southeast of Hyderabad.

Thanks to the work of the foundation, people no longer have to walk to Bhimavaram city for medicines. The stock of free medications for diabetes, blood pressure and other health conditions is readily available at the foundation's medical camps. Ambulances are only a call away. The foundation also made contributions to education and drinking water in several villages in the coastal districts. It established 50 water purification plants that catered to almost 200 villages. The locals sang praises of the positive impact the foundation had on them.[1]

Raju may be a white-collar bad boy for the world, but he is seen as a Good Samaritan in his state. In 2009, several villagers

---

[1]Mahapatra, Rajesh, 'Satyam Scam: Village Mourns and Prays for Raju', *Hindustan Times*, 16 January 2009, https://bit.ly/3RzZJmu. Accessed on 15 July 2022.

in coastal Andhra refused to celebrate Sankranti, one of South India's most popular harvest festivals. The famous cockfights, the card games and the usual fanfare were missing as families slipped into mourning at Raju's arrest. None of them either understood or wanted to understand the crime. To them, Raju was the God who could never fail.[2]

The city-bred may have lost their equity investment in Satyam because of him, but the villagers were sure their Gaaru (akin to sir) would come clean, smelling of roses.

Back in the office, the bond Raju developed with the workforce and the reverence they had for him were unparalleled. First, he was a generous boss. At Satyam, each vertical operated as a silo, and if you were a business leader, you had great independence. No one encroached on your operation; neither did they bother you with what others were doing in their fiefdom. This suited them admirably, as each worked like a strategic business unit. Later, these same silos meant that nobody at the leadership knew the overall financials and real profits. As many of the senior leaders told me in our personal interactions, they joined Satyam in the 1990s and stayed with it because of the respect with which they were treated.

The leaders, their families and the top management met annually over dinner. Family members moved freely with each other, including those of the promoters and directors. Camaraderie flowed, and Raju came across as a pleasant and honest man. In those get-togethers, everyone was surprised by his down-to-earth and soft-spoken attitude. The news of Raju's confession shook the executives, and the women and children in their families. They were deeply saddened, as if one of their own family members had been imprisoned.

During my days in Satyam, Ramulu, a seasoned and dedicated soul, chauffeured me. He said that in his long career

---

[2]Ibid.

as Raju's regular driver, he had never seen the chairman raise his voice. Others told me that Raju would just close his eyes for a few seconds when faced with an adverse situation and then open them. Afterwards, he would focus on what needed to be done instead of worrying about what had happened.

However, beyond all these, his claim to fame, without a shadow of a doubt, was the Emergency Management and Research Institute (EMRI).

◆

The EMRI, better known as 108 Service, changed how emergency medical care is delivered in India. And, if one man deserves kudos for that, it is the man whose business card read 'Byrraju Ramalinga Raju'. The number '108' is modelled after 911, the US's signature emergency number. It brings emergency care to anyone, irrespective of caste and religion, regardless of wealth or poverty.

Before the arrival of 108, about four million Indians died every year due to inadequate medical emergency services. Of the four million, 60 per cent (2.4 million) were related to cardiac emergencies.[3] Next, you had multiple helpline numbers, and in a crisis, no one remembered which one to call. Today, in 18 states we know we must call 108, wherever we are, whoever we are and whichever hospital we wish to be in.

EMRI's ambulances are not mere transport vehicles. Raju standardized them, made them offer pre-hospital care and provided the service free of charge. He contributed ₹34 crore towards the initial corpus, with which the EMRI building was built, hardware for a call centre obtained and the purchase

---

[3]Wangchuk, Rinchen Norbu, 'Calling 108: How One Institution Pioneered Emergency Medical Services in India', *The Better India*, 4 July 2019, https://bit.ly/3clOJcb. Accessed on 19 July 2022.

of the first 30 ambulances made.[4]

The journey kicked off on Independence Day of 2005, and Andhra Pradesh Chief Minister Y.S.R. Reddy flagged it off. The EMRI signed a service contract with the state government. A year later, Raju launched another 40 ambulances, taking the tally to 70 in the Telugu state. Seeing EMRI's success, the Andhra government, in August 2007, decided to become a financial partner and funded 95 per cent of the operation, which meant 700 ambulances were pressed into service that month. Raju's philanthropy was working.

So, how does 108 operate? Anyone, anywhere, in any street of Andhra Pradesh, facing an emergency, has to dial in 108 from any telephone device. At the first ring, the phone is picked at the dedicated EMRI centre in Hyderabad. An executive speaks to the caller, gathers the needed information and identifies the problem. If it is medical, the call is channelized to the medical centre. If related to law and order, it is passed on to the police personnel. And if it's a fire, the nearest fire station is alerted.

The system then quickly pairs caller numbers with a physical address and assigns the ambulance, police squad or fire engine as the case may be. For medical emergencies, the ambulance is equipped with a stretcher and is well stocked with medicines, oxygen and a first-aid box. Both the driver and the attendant are trained for handling any situation. The medical attendant gets in touch with the caller while on the move and gives them instructions for preliminary care. The ambulance usually arrives at the venue within 15 minutes from the call time, when the attendants take over to provide first aid. A simultaneous online consultation is provided from the EMRI. Similarly, if the issue relates to law and order, the police van reaches the spot and attends to the problem. The EMRI has provided immense relief, especially in accident cases, as

---

[4]Ibid.

before 108, people had difficulty in getting medical attention from private hospitals and the police found it challenging, too. The rigours of fulfilling legal formalities have been taken over by the EMRI. In fact, the police force loves the EMRI facility, I was told.

The Rajus contributed to building infrastructure, providing technological support, owning and operating ambulances, and bringing in appropriate human resources in doctors, police and support-services teams. Yet, in the entire infrastructure, neither the promoters' name nor photograph appears. What's also remarkable is that a global positioning system (GPS) was put in place which could track the nearest ambulance location and the most relevant hospital when India did not even have a standard GPS in place!

Thank you, Raju.

So, why did Raju choose the number 108?

At that time, '100' was earmarked for the public to avail the services of the police. '101' was the number to call the ambulance. '108' was also in the pipeline but was not used. The government was willing to give 108 for this new initiative, and Raju took it.

It is well known that 108 service created a revolutionary impact among people. Several state governments cottoned on to the idea. Nine states had it implemented, and two others signed the Memorandum of Understanding (MoU) in 2008. Today, EMRI is run throughout India as a public–private partnership between state governments and private emergency medical services.

However, apart from this practical consideration, the number 108 also has a religious connotation and a scientific significance. Mantras usually are recited 108 times and measured with 108 beads in the mala. Scientifically, the sun's diameter is about 108 times that of the earth's. And the midpoint between the earth and the sun is 108 times the sun's diameter. Finally, the average distance from the earth to the moon is about 108 times the moon's diameter.

◆

The state was also suffering a shortage of Primary Healthcare Centres and Community Healthcare Centres, which meant lower-quality care for its citizens. Raju founded the Health Management and Research Institute (HMRI 104) as an NGO. Dr Balaji Utla was made its CEO in addition to being vice chairman, Satyam Foundation.

The HMRI programme is for the rural poor who had limited access to medical doctors. A person can dial the toll free 104 number and avail free medical advice from healthcare professionals managed by the HMRI. Assisted by a pre-formatted algorithm, callers are matched with qualified health workers, including medical speciality experts, for advice or to make preliminary diagnoses and referrals. Calls are prioritized and routed to appropriate destinations, including 108 if an ambulance is required.

Dr Utla was heading the Learning Centre at Satyam before moving out to HMRI. In his discussions with Dr Utla, Raju found out that the HMRI provides healthcare to 3.5 million people. The annual expenditure was ₹270–280 crore. Of this, the Andhra government bore 95 per cent, and Raju contributed the remaining 5 per cent. Raju also provided technical support for the dial-in access through 104. In 2006, the Andhra Pradesh finance minister Konijeti Rosaiah inaugurated the dial-in 104 facility. Dr Rosaiah became the state's chief minister and later the governor of the neighbouring Tamil Nadu and Karnataka.

The fact that both EMRI and HMRI have gone national is a testimony to Ramalinga Raju's vision.

◆

Last on the list is Satyam Foundation. In 2001, Satyam set it up with three trustees: Nandini, Radha and Sundari. Nandini was married to Chairman Ramalinga Raju and Radha to Managing Director B. Rama Raju, while Sundari was married to A.S. Murthy. Murthy, who helmed HR in 2001, and later became head of Global Delivery and Leadership Development, would rise to be the interim CEO during the crisis-laden 100 days.

The purpose of the foundation was to get Satyam employees to run social responsibility programmes for urban renewal through volunteerism. The activities were funded by collecting ₹20 per month from all Indian employees and a quarterly contribution from Satyam at 0.25 per cent of its profit before tax.

The foundation, headed by Naveen Yelloji as director and CEO, focussed on four principal areas of work: Education and Livelihood, Social and Preventive Healthcare, Vulnerable Social Groups, and Environment.

The foundation's activities generated considerable goodwill for Satyam, especially among overseas customers, as multinational corporations (MNCs) prefer to deal with socially conscious companies. The foundation also surely gave enormous fulfilment to Satyamites, who pitched in with their share of contribution.

◆

When Raju confessed to his shenanigans, it looked like his philanthropic activities might fall apart. Although he ring-fenced the entities with participation from the government, many high-profile resignations happened on the board of EMRI.

The first to go was former president Dr A.P.J. Abdul Kalam. Others followed. The iconic K.V. Kamath of ICICI Bank left. It was logical for Kiran Karnik and Tarun Das as members of the newly appointed Satyam-board to resign. Krishna Palepu of Harvard Business School, a former independent director of Satyam, was once bitten twice shy. B. Rama Raju, once managing director of Satyam, obviously had to quit.

However, a few directors stayed back, and rightly so. These included Jayaprakash Narayan, the political analyst, Krishnam Raju, the industrialist, Prof. Raj Reddy of Carnegie Mellon University and Rajat Gupta, the then ISB board chairman. They held the fort until the government announced a takeover.

On Saturday, 11 April, I visited the EMRI facility and was utterly bowled over. I met Venkat Changavalli, the institution's CEO and backbone, and spent half a day going around the facility and admiring every facet of the live operation. One has to see to believe. Venkat passionately narrated the journey of EMRI and how it took off across India. On three occasions, this engineer and IIM alumnus emotionally broke down while referring to Raju's benevolence in building the institution. It was amazing to see such an institution built and run, touching millions of Indian lives.

I was moved by the indelible impact Raju left on all those who worked closely with him. Venkat also told me that immediately after being taken into custody, Raju spoke to him and insisted that come what may, EMRI should never be discontinued, even if Satyam fell.

This was Ramalinga Raju, in his Dr Henry Jekyll avatar from Robert Louis Stevenson's novella, *The Strange Case of Dr Jekyll and Mr Hyde*. He had two distinct faces. Alas, in the real world, they do not neutralize each other. We don't have to worry about which was the real Raju, because he was both. Perhaps it would be best to say that he was Mr Hyde by circumstance and Dr Jekyll by nature.

◆

CREATING VALUE FOR SOCIETY*

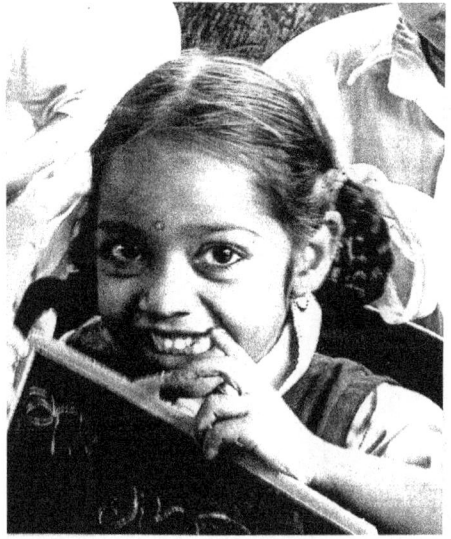

At Satyam, we are committed to giving back to the society that we live and work in. This spirit of fellowship drives our corporate social responsibility. We expect all our associates to be empathetic to Society's needs and indeed, encourage them to spend 10% of their time on helping those less-privileged. We have the largest corporate volunteering program amongst all corporations in India.

Satyam Foundation supports and strengthens the vulnerable and underprivileged sections in urban areas for transforming the quality of life through technology and volunteerism.

Amongst the solutions enabled by Satyam leaders, are the IT backbones for Emergency Research Management Institute (EMRI) and Health Management and Research Institute (HMRI). EMRI is a 108, single number service that provides critical public emergency management and services. EMRI's vision is to provide leadership, resources and support to respond to 1 million calls each day and to save one million lives a year nationally, by 2010.

HMRI is a public-private partnership with the Government of Andhra Pradesh that aims to augment health delivery systems in the state. As part of this, HMRI has implemented a 24x7 Health Helpline serving the eighty million people of Andhra Pradesh.

---

*From Satyam's 21st Annual Report (pp. 16–17). This is for the year 2007–08 and is the last financial statement signed by the Rajus.

MALATHI

"At the end of the training, I was confident for the first time in life that I would be able to take care of my child and myself. Though I know that, I will not be cured of the virus, with due care and proper medication, I will be able to live longer and see my child grow. My child is healthy, free of the HIV virus and is going to school. Thank you, Satyam Foundation for helping me reclaim my life."

VENKAT RAMANA

"I used to think that I will keep struggling like my father and would not be able to change things. Satyam Foundation helped me to break free and realize my potential. I joined the IT school run by the foundation, where I learnt spoken English, improved my communication skills and also picked up some computer skills. After the course, I applied for and won a job as a computer operator in Kuwait."

PART 4

RESCUE BEGINS

7

STRATEGY AND FUNDING

I returned to Hyderabad on 19 January.

At the Satyam headquarters, like any other senior employee, I occupied an earmarked cabin in the Infocity campus. For the first time in my 25-year career, I began working as a corporate honcho. I took time to understand the work. Sometimes, senior associates dropped by to assist. I often walked around to meet up with associates and to get to know them. I also used to explain their role in the revival process. I recalled years ago my reading the seminal author Tom Peters's writing about 'management by walking around'. Now I was practising it!

I interacted with each team member to gather their view of the ground reality and their suggestions on the board's measures. I interacted with finance, legal, secretarial and corporate services. It was gratifying that Company Secretary Jayaraman, well assisted by V.S.N. Raju and S. Raji Reddy, was doing an adequate job of monitoring global compliance and ensuring timely regulatory filings. I sat with the internal audit team to understand the status of their work and its transition to Brahmayya & Co.

Next, I had discussions with Satyam BPO, our subsidiary, on how to increase revenue and drive cost reduction. Chief Operating Officer (COO) Vijay Rangineni explained the financial and operational issues while Company Secretary (Satyam BPO), Tushar Chudgar, briefed me on the compliance.

Instead of sipping coffee or tea during breaks, I opened the window to take in a breath of fresh air. As I looked at the plants growing alongside Satyam's compound, I wondered how tall they would be by the time we revived the company. When the plants waved in the breeze, I felt like they were trying to cheer me up!

I took customer calls at the office. However, I took the US calls from the guesthouse because they were scheduled either at midnight or early in the morning, Indian Standard Time (IST).

Over the next 12 weeks, a feeling kept nagging me. Raju had set up a world-class infrastructure, groomed a premium talent pool and built an elite portfolio of customers. Now, the future of all this was at stake due to the weight of the billion-plus-dollar scandal. What was lost in the course of the fraud was the reputation painstakingly built over the past two decades.

I also worried about India's reputation and the possibility of job loss. I told myself that the priority was to separate the good from the bad. The good represented the company, the employees and the customers who needed to be protected, and their interests preserved. The bad represented those who defrauded the company, and they were best left to be handled by the investigators. We owed them nothing.

The thought that all this would resurrect the nation's image was energizing.

What should we do to put things back on track? What should we do to remove the stain of the scandal? These thoughts would plague me till I found a solution.

◆

On the night of 20 January 2009, I watched on television Barack Obama deliver his historic address on assuming office as president.[1]

---

[1] 'President Barack Obama's Inaugural Address', The White House: President Barack Obama, 21 January 2009, https://bit.ly/3RLKAhM. Accessed on 19 July 2022.

'*I stand here today humbled by the task before us, grateful for the trust you've bestowed, mindful of the sacrifices borne by our ancestors,*' the first African-American president said. Humbled. Trust. These rang a bell.

'*Today I say to you that the challenges we face are real... They will not be met easily or in a short span of time. But know this, America: They will be met.*' I could relate those words to the challenges in Satyam.

'*On this day, we gather because we have chosen hope over fear, unity of purpose over conflict and discord.*' So apt for the Satyamites to join hands with us.

'*We will build the roads and bridges, the electric grids and digital lines that feed our commerce and bind us together. We'll restore science to its rightful place and wield technology's wonders to raise health care's quality and lower its cost.*' How wonderful it would be if we, the board, could be the pathway that leads to Satyam's revival.

'*Let it be said by our children's children that when we were tested, we refused to let this journey end, that we did not turn back nor did we falter; and with eyes fixed on the horizon and God's grace upon us, we carried forth that great gift of freedom and delivered it safely to future generations.*' These final words were chilling. I pledged to my conscience that we would use the freedom given to us by the government and deliver on the mandate to resurrect the company.

Unwittingly, I told myself, 'Yes, we can.' Nobody heard, but that did not matter. I had heard it; that's all that mattered.

◆

The government-nominated team's third board meeting was held on 22 January, Thursday, and 23 January, Friday. The suave Padma Bhushan awardee, Tarun Das, a former member of the International Advisory Board of Coca-Cola, chaired it. It was an important meeting, as we had to decide several aspects on which the revival plan hinged.

The most important of them all was to find a strategic investor for the company who could bring in capital and take control of the operations of the company. In contrast, a financial investor merely brings in money and leaves the conduct of business to the existing management.

We knew someday we had to step aside. We weren't going to babysit forever. After all, our mandate was to handhold the company and then hand it over to a strategic investor. The deliberation was on how to do it and how soon.

We had two options before us.

OPTION 1: SHELL COMPANY

The first was to keep Satyam as a shell company—a corporation that exists only on paper, has minimal or no employees and almost no operations. Among its several purposes, a legitimate cause for creating a shell company is to transfer assets from one company into a new one and leave the liabilities in the former company. We examined this route as an option.

We thought it would be a good idea to sell Satyam's business, namely its assets and ongoing contracts, for consideration and keep all of its liabilities and claims in Satyam as a shell entity. The investor would then carry out the business in their brand name without the headache of class-action suits and other litigations, even as Satyam would face the cases.

The investor would get a rich talent pool, an enviable client-base and world-class infrastructure for their money. We expected them to queue up and pay a handsome price, as the acquisition would be free of Satyam's tarnished tag and of its current and potential liabilities. The new entity would focus on business, while Satyam concentrated on fighting claims and settling disputes. With a small staff, a thin board and the significant consideration received from the investor, Satyam could comfortably pay off its liabilities. The remaining money would be disbursed to shareholders. Afterwards, the company would be wound up.

With this, a fabled story would end. Satyam would go to its corporate grave with an engraving on its tombstone—B: 1987. D: 2009.

There were several reasons why this option didn't fly. Some of them were moral, some psychological, others were practical and some others financial.

For instance, the sale would lead to substantial capital gains tax at the hands of Satyam, thereby reducing cash availability. Next, it could be practically tricky to transfer assets due to the many conditions attached to Satyam properties. Further, there was no guarantee that either the customers or associates would work with the new masters at an emotional level. The challenge of reviving the company would not be there for associates, and they may seek greener pasture.

What finally dealt a death knell to this idea was a genuine belief that if we went through this process, there was a greater probability Satyam would lose the claims and cases against it.

Moreover, knowing Satyam was now no one's baby, every Tom, Dick and Harry would swoop down to make claims. The sale money would enhance Satyam's ability to settle, reduce its bargaining power and the company would lose the sympathy factor. In the end, its shareholders may get nothing worthwhile upon liquidation. We believed we owed a moral obligation to shareholders. Also, at a psychological level, no one wanted a corporate death.

OPTION 2: SHARES TO NEW INVESTOR

The second option was to make a preferential allotment of Satyam shares to a new investor at a competitive price fixed in an open auction. The buyer would infuse capital and take a controlling interest in the company. The new owner would participate in the pleasures and pains, and the assets and the liabilities, both known and unknown. Thus, Satyam, as an entity, would stay.

The money that the investor brought would not be the result of a sale but a fresh infusion of capital. So, there would be no cash outflow towards tax. Of course, some corporate law and SEBI requirements would have to be met, but that was okay. The new promoters would rehabilitate the business by paying off banks, vendors and service providers and settling court cases.

Given the above analysis, we chose the second option. This way, the revival process had logic to back it. The forensic investigation would be continued and completed to facilitate the restatement of accounts and clean up all notional amounts earlier recorded in the books. The SEC requirements would thus be complied with. Similarly, the needs of India's stock market regulator SEBI would be met. This would enable Satyam to tap into unexplored opportunities associated with its strengths, overcome its weaknesses and surmount its threats resulting in a holistic turnaround. Stripping the assets and selling these lock, stock and barrel would have looked like a real estate transaction and not a clean, corporate turnaround!

ALTERNATIVES IN OPTION 2

If we thought that with this, the strategizing was over, we were wrong. We still had to decide how and when to bring in the new investor.

Should we run Satyam as a government-administered company for a year, by which time accounts would be restated for the previous six years, financial stability established, a forensic audit carried out and all legal tangles smoothened out? After that, should we offer due diligence and valuation exercises to be carried out and go in for sale as a going concern by showcasing Satyam with its natural strengths and assets? This was one alternative.

The second alternative was to focus on the revival of business, initiate actions for a restatement of accounts, forensic investigations, defend cases and claims, and quickly announce an offer for the acquisition of controlling interest as a going concern. Towards this, appoint investment bankers, move the regulators and judicial forums for necessary relaxations and approvals and kick-start the takeover process to be completed over the next few months. The takeover would be on an as-is-where-is basis. Once a new strategic investor was identified, we could handhold it for a few months until the new management got a grip on things.

The overarching view in the boardroom was that any delay in bringing in a new owner might lead to the business's deterioration. We felt that unless customers saw new owners emerging, they would move out.

In the IT industry, unlike a brick-and-mortar industry, it is, no doubt, demanding for a customer to migrate to an alternative service provider within three to four months. But beyond that, it is possible to migrate seamlessly. Even if there was no team with the relevant domain expertise, the customer could ask us to transfer the entire squad to their payroll or the competitor's. If that happened, Satyam would lose not only the customers but also the employees. In that eventuality, Satyam's business would collapse like a pack of cards, and we would be left only with the real estate.

It was, therefore, crucial that we quickly bring in a new owner.

The other fear was the possibility of the customers considering us a government enterprise. Technology companies are private players abroad, and the perception that Satyam was a government entity could rob it of its sheen. This also contributed to our decision to opt for the second alternative in Option 2 and find a strategic investor.

Once we made up our minds, Deepak began to identify investment bankers.

That day, at lunchtime, we surprised Deepak by requesting him to cut a cake. CNBC TV 18 had adjudged him the 'Outstanding Business Leader' of 2008. We saw it as a happy omen towards Satyam's revival. Along with Jayaraman and a few members of the leadership team, the board was present.

◆

In the interregnum, to meet operational expenses, the board had requested Deepak to speak to bankers to identify those willing to lend to Satyam. Later in the day, he suggested we approach IDBI and Bank of Baroda (BoB) for ₹300 crore each and said they had, in principle, consented to lend. The necessary formalities in terms of getting the documentation done began in right earnest. Simultaneously, the board wanted the leadership team not to depend on any likely sanction of loans but to expedite customer collections and execute cost optimization measures.

We decided to maintain a fresh set of books of accounts from 10 January 2009.

On the sidelines of this board meeting, Kiran and Tarun attended to calls and briefed customers such as GSK, Applied Materials, CISCO and Coke on the revival plan. Kiran spoke to Gartner. The board decided to send personalized emails to all key customers articulating positive developments.

On 22 January, we had a surprise visitor. Price Waterhouse, represented by its chairman Ramesh Rajan, partners Thomas and Deepak, Indian counsel Soma Sekhar, accompanied by their US Counsel, met the board. They informed that the letter dated 13 January, withdrawing reliance on their audit report, was as per Section 10(A) of the US Securities and Exchange Commission Act, 1934. They said the restated accounts needed to be audited and certified by PW as the company's statutory auditors and expressed interest in continuing the services. We promised to get back to them after taking stock of the situation.

The need never arose as PW resigned on 12 February. The board took note of this in its meeting of 21 February. It was the logical thing to do, given that the SEC in the US and SEBI in India were investigating the matter and could possibly initiate action against them. Meanwhile, their partners were also under the scanner of ICAI for possible disciplinary action. Under the circumstances, their continuation was untenable.

Meanwhile, the board approved various petitions and applications prepared by Cyril Amarchand Mangaldas to be filed before SEBI, the finance ministry and the CLB seeking immunities and exceptions. This was done so that the past wrongs were not attributed to us, the new board. We requested it to make necessary recommendations to the central government under Sections 230 and 24B of the SEBI Act. Further, drawing reference to the MoU between SEBI and SEC dated 6 May 1998, and according to the International Organization of Securities Commissions executed as a multilateral MoU in May 2002, we requested SEBI to write to SEC for similar immunity for us under the US Securities Laws.

The second was an application to the Takeover Panel of SEBI seeking exemption from the application of Regulation 20(4) of the Takeover Code.

In light of Raju's confession and the disclaimer on the reliability of their audit by PW, the trading prices of Satyam shares before 7 January 2009 were not representative of their actual value. The fact that the stock was withdrawn from Sensex and Nifty added credence to our claim. We wanted to ignore the statutory practice of considering prices during the previous 26 weeks for considering averages under Regulation 20(4) of the Takeover Code. We suggested competitive bid-based best offers be permitted.

The next application was to the MCA for immunities under the Companies Act, 1956, the Securities and Exchange Board of India Act, 1992, and the Securities Contracts (Regulation) Act, 1956. As our appointment was under Section 388C(2) and Section 403 of the Companies Act, we were officers of the court. We wanted protection from the consequences of any wrongdoings of the previous management. Our legal advisors suggested this to us.

A petition was made to the CLB to grant immunity to the board members under Section 403 of the Companies Act, 1956, so no agency initiated any action against us for the previous board's omissions and commissions. We also wanted the CLB to protect the company's actions, such as availing loans and creating security. Real and imaginary creditors were suing Satyam in various courts and asking the directors not to alienate or deal with the assets. They even threatened to hold directors personally liable for such actions. An example was a letter dated 7 January 2009, from Upaid Systems, an erstwhile customer of a Satyam subsidiary. The board looked at raising money, and lenders would give loans only against adequate security in Satyam's assets. Hence, we sought explicit sanction from the CLB.

The crux of all these filings was that we apprehended possible proceedings against us under various laws. So, we moved the above petitions for immunity for the six of us during our functioning as board members. We needed to feel comfortable discharging our functions without pulling the weight of the past board's civil or criminal actions.

When the meeting concluded, Tarun told the media that the associates continued to show remarkable resilience and exceptional commitment towards the company during these challenging times. Kiran said, 'There is a pronounced shift in customer attitudes from being alarmed in the initial days;

it has changed to a sense of cautious optimism.'[2]

Answering some of the questions raised about the company's headcount by a few external authorities, the board confirmed prima facie that there appeared to be no basis to doubt the same.

At Satyam, regular employees and contract workers (45,297), people on subsidiaries' payroll (4,075) and direct billing force (1,628) added up to 51,000 as of 12 January 2009. An e-support password change was mandatory every 60 days. An e-support portal needs to be accessed for leave, travel, reimbursements, appraisals, salary revision letters, surveys, immigration, insurance, procurement requests, etc. Associates who changed passwords in November 2008–January 2009, including those exempted for password change, accounted for 45,297. In the past 15 days alone, 43,947 associates (out of 45,297) logged on to the e-support application. A few days later, Deloitte reaffirmed there were no ghosts on the rolls.

The board decided to meet informally on 26 January and formally on 27 January to conclude some of the other compelling items on the agenda. After that, all the board colleagues left Hyderabad for their respective destinations.

Having founded a CA firm back in 1984, I am used to working six days a week and sometimes even on a Sunday on a need basis. But in the IT industry, five days a week was the norm, so religiously adhered to across all locations of Satyam, that even if I wanted to sit in Hyderabad and work, no one would be available!

◆

Usually, in informal meetings, Deepak would lay down certain strategic moves for our comments. Apparently, he conceived

---

[2]Singh, Praveen Kumar, 'Client Exits Threaten Satyam's Valuation', *The Indian Express*, 30 January 2009, https://bit.ly/3yNmb32. Accessed on 19 July 2022.

them on the flight, and it was fascinating to see how he predicted things and proactively put mitigating measures in place.

We decided to raise stopgap working capital. We needed this loan for two reasons. One, if our collections didn't come on time to meet our salary obligations, we could use this money. Two, even if the collections were adequate, they would flow into different bank accounts in different geographies, and pooling them in one place to disburse payment would be cumbersome. IDBI and BoB were willing to step in to lend, provided we got a no objection certificate from the Andhra Pradesh Industrial Infrastructure Corporation (APIIC). This was because we were mortgaging the Hi-Tech City property allotted to Satyam by the government through APIIC.

Deepak told us two investment bankers—Goldman Sachs and Avendus—had been invited to make a presentation to the board on the 27th, after which we could take a call on appointing them to advise the board on strategic options.

During such a discussion, an SEC requirement was brought to our notice. It appears that in the case of a US-listed company, a whole-time director and CEO position should be filled within 15 days of the vacancy arising.

Deepak suggested, 'Manoharan, anyway you have decided to spend full time on Satyam. So, why don't you be the whole-time director?' Other colleagues promptly endorsed his view. It was heartening they reposed so much faith in me when I had never worked with any of them in the past. I said, 'I need to ponder about this idea and will let you all know tomorrow.'

On 27 January, over breakfast, I said, 'I will do the job of a whole-time director but without the designation.' When their eyebrows rose curiously, I said, 'The moment the board announces my name as the whole-time director, the entire spotlight will shift on me and the media will hound me. I am averse to both and want to work without distraction.'

To their everlasting credit, the board understood my point

of view. Deepak said we could ask our US counsel to get more time to fill the vacancy.

A few minutes later, Tarun came to me, smiled and said, 'The world will not know what you are doing on a full-time basis.' I returned his smile, 'Tarun, I am not doing this for the world to know. I am doing this for my nation, my profession and my satisfaction.'

His pat and his words indicated he liked and supported my response.

◆

At the fourth meeting of the government-nominated board on 27 January, I was elected as the chairman. It was a privilege chairing this board, which had so many luminaries.

We received a disclosure from Larsen & Toubro (L&T), indicating they had increased their stake in Satyam from 4.48 per cent to 12.04 per cent. I wondered if this was a vote of confidence.

We noted that current outstanding fund-based loans, including exposure to foreign exchange derivatives and non-fund-based limits towards guarantees and Letters of Credit were about ₹750 crore.

Cyril Amarchand Mangaldas told us it had shortlisted Wachtell, Lipton, Rosen & Katz (New York) as legal counsel for handling class-action suits in the US, and they could negotiate for a fee of $1,50,000 per month as against the standard fee of $3,00,000 per month. A senior partner would be available for the company, they added. The board approved it. We also decided to retain Latham & Watkins to attend to the SEC's statutory filings and regulatory dialogue with SEC/NYSE.

The board appointed the Boston Consulting Group (BCG) as management advisors to support the directors and the Satyam leadership team. A dedicated three-member senior team from BCG would work closely with the board during this revival process. The firm deployed James Abraham (senior partner and managing director) and Ashish Iyer (partner and director). Arun Maira (senior advisor) also joined the team to guide on governance and communication.

'An important point to note is they will not be charging Satyam any fees for their services, and this reflects on their commitment to the task on hand,' Deepak told the media.[3]

The board announced Goldman Sachs and Avendus as investment bankers to advise the company on strategic options in finding a potential suitor. These options included identifying strategic investors, obtaining expressions of interest, and ensuring a fair and transparent approach to the entire process.

I told the media,

> The board has received several proposals from corporate entities as well as from select PE firms. Some have shown interest in evaluating Satyam as an integrated entity, while others have expressed interest in Satyam's business portions. A sale of 'parts' is contrary to the mandate of regulating Satyam's affairs as a going concern, as stipulated by the Government of India. It is, therefore, not an option that is being evaluated currently.[4]

The question of L&T buying a significant stake in Satyam in the open market came up. I told the media that the question of why L&T was acquiring a bigger stake should be directed at the construction major. I also said this did not mean we were supporting a takeover by L&T. Instead, we were working with SEBI and the central government to enable open bids. I believed these actions reassured our march towards stability.

◆

---

[3]'Salaries Will Be Paid on Time, Says Satyam Board', *The Indian Express*, 28 January 2009, https://bit.ly/3aMh7nk. Accessed on 19 July 2022.
[4]Ibid.

After the meeting on 27 January, while my co-directors left, I stayed back in Hyderabad. The following day was hectic. I spoke to Citibank to enable the release of salaries. I talked to BNP Paribas to finalize the modified terms. I wrote to IDBI and BoB, indicating the broad terms for the new loans to be sanctioned. IDBI wanted to do a title verification of the properties of Satyam. As we gave an equitable mortgage of two prime properties, I suggested avoiding a charge on receivables.

Somewhere around this time, the Regional Provident Fund Commissioner threatened to file an FIR for non-payment of employees' contributions deducted from their salary. I spoke to Commissioner M. Vijayaraj and explained that the old management was no longer in control of affairs. I told him that the government-appointed board was sorting out the defaults. He was gracious enough to give us some time but wanted an early closure, failing which, he would not be able to stop the consequences.

V.V.K. Raju, a senior vice president, informed me that the commercial taxes department had raised a demand for ₹5.5 crore towards sales tax arrears and indicated that our bank accounts would be attached if payments were not made. I spoke to the commissioner and persuaded him to accept a down payment of ₹50 lakh and keep recovery proceedings pending until the appeals were disposed. We had done something similar with the Income Tax Department.

I informed our legal advisors about the threat from PF authorities. I then coordinated with Pallavi Shroff, who confirmed filing the petition before the CLB, seeking board members' immunity.

Both director Achuthan and lawyer Shardul Shroff went to SEBI in Mumbai to move petitions approved in the board meeting held on 23 January relating to takeover concessions.

On 29 January, we received an order from CLB granting us immunity and clarifying that the board had powers to raise loans even by creating a charge on the company's movable and immovable property. This immunity applied to all the functionaries who had been or were likely to be appointed by the present board. The CLB also said the government-nominated directors were like court officers, and therefore, every state or central government entity must support them in their endeavours.

This development was a shot in our arm and sent a positive message about how serious the government and the CLB were about reviving Satyam.

◆

CLB Order Dated 29 January 2009: Granting Immunity Order by S. Balasubramanian, Chairman of the CLB

BEFORE THE COMPANY LAW BOARD
PRINCIPAL BENCH
NEW DELHI
(Dated: 29th January 2009)

CP No. 001 of 2009
CA No.40/09

Present: Shri S. Balasubramanian,
Chairman

In the matter of Companies Act, 1956-Sections 388B/397/398/408
AND
In the matter of Union of India
versus
Satyam Computer Services Limited & others.

Petitioner:
Union of India, New Delhi
Respondents:
1. M/s Satyam Computer Services Ltd.
2. Shri Ramalinga Raju - Chairman
3. Shri B. Rama Raju - MD
4. Shri Rammohan Rao Mynampati - WTD
5. Shri Mangalam Srinivasan
6. Shri Krishna G.Palepu
7. Shri Vinod K. Dham
8. Shri M.Rammohan Rao
9. Shri V.S.Raju
10. Shri T.R.Prasad
11. M/s Price Waterhouse,.CAs, Auditors of the company
12. Shri G.Jayaraman, Company Secretary

Present on behalf of parties:
1. Mr. Sanjay Shorey, DD (I)   ... for Petitioner
2. Ms. Pallavi S.Shroff, Advocate   ... for Respondent No.1
3. Ms. Ritu Bhalla, Advocate   ... for Respondent No.1
4. Ms. Jasleen K.Oberoi, Advocate   ... for Respondent No.1

ORDER

1. The instant application has been filed by the company seeking for various interim reliefs on the grounds stated in the application.

2. Heard on the application. Satyam episode does not require any elaboration. With the view to protect the interests of the company, its large workforce, customers and more so, in the larger public interest, the Union of India, invoked various provisions of the companies Act before this Board and sought for urgent ex-parte interim reliefs. Forming a prima facie opinion that there existed sufficient grounds to exercise the powers of this Board under Section 403 of the Act, to regulate the affairs of the company, by an order dated 9.1.2009, while suspending the then existing Board of Directors, I also authorized the Union of India to appoint, in the name and on behalf of this Board not more than 10 eminent persons as directors of the company. Accordingly, the Central Government has appointed, for the time being, 6 eminent persons as directors. Since, they have been appointed in the name and on behalf of this Board, they are like court officers and therefore every state or central government entity is bound to assist and support them in their endeavours, more so, when they have joined the Board as a measure of public service.

3. However, ignoring the larger public interest involved in their assuming the onerous responsibility of reviving the troubled company, PF authorities have threatened to initiate action against the directors, which action is not sustainable. Therefore, I restrain the PF authorities from initiating any action against the present directors of the company without the leave of this Board, more so in respect of omissions, commissions and/or default on the part of the suspended board of directors. To ensure that the present Board of directors discharges its function without any apprehension of being subjected to civil, criminal or punitive action, I direct that none of the State or Central Government agencies shall, in exercise of their regulatory, enforcement or like such powers, initiate any action, civil, criminal, punitive, coercive against the present directors in discharge of their collective or individual responsibilities, without the prior leave of this Board. This direction is applicable to all the functionaries that have been or likely to be appointed by the present board. However, the Board of Directors, shall cooperate with the concerned agencies as may be necessary, whenever any information or documents are required by these agencies.

4. Since as per my order dated 9.1.2009 the board has been authorized to exercise and discharge all powers as per the articles and the Act, this authorization is applicable to rising of finances in the form of loan or otherwise and also to mortgage, charge and encumber any of the movable and immovable assets of the company including providing them as securities, if need be.

5. The Central Government shall endorse a copy of this order to all the Central Ministries for circulation to their subordinate regulatory, enforcement agencies for their information. Like wise a copy of this order be endorsed to the Government of Andra Pradesh also for such circulation amongst the state agencies.

Sd/-
(S. BALASUBRAMANIAN)

V. N. SHARMA
Bench Officer
Company Law Board
New Delhi

8

NAVIGATING THROUGH TURBULENCE

After qualifying as a CA in 1983, I keenly attended seminars as part of continuing professional education. I started teaching in 1988, and began presenting papers in seminars, workshops and conferences in 1989. I travelled across India and overseas to address programmes organized by various forums, notably the ICAI, its regional councils, branches and overseas chapters.

I was scheduled to visit Bahrain on 30 and 31 January 2009 for some ICAI work. The engagement had been fixed before my appointment to the Satyam board. I had consented to present a paper and deliver the keynote address at the valedictory session of an international conference organized by the Bahrain Chapter of ICAI. I felt this trip's substantial time, except when participating in my sessions, must be devoted to meeting Satyam's clients and motivating Satyamites who worked in Bahrain.

In Bahrain, I met Satyam's associates, Fayez Ramzy Fayez and Souvik Dey, to understand the status of client projects. The country was then a significant banking hub for the Middle East. Satyam was servicing Bank Muscat International (BMI) on a $20 million contract. I learnt from the executives that BMI was hesitant to continue with us and was exploring alternative service channels. We fixed an appointment and had an hour-long conversation with CEO Andrew Bainbridge and COO Marco Peter Wolters.

Andrew wanted to be briefed about the crisis before allowing the Satyam team to continue with the work. I explained the government's initiatives and the board's measures and resolved all of their apprehensions. Marco wanted the contract to be amended before releasing the $5,00,000 due to Satyam. He wanted a bank guarantee equivalent to liquidated damages and also to further stagger the payments based on stringent measurement of completion of milestones. I negotiated and agreed for partial modifications and left for the hotel, happy we had not lost a client.

The next customer visit was to Bahrain Telecommunications Co. (Batelco), a leading player in the telecom space, akin to India's Reliance. The experience was in stark contrast to BMI and for valid reasons. Here, Satyam was asked to get ready to pack its bags. I was shocked our associates had approached the client, seeking advance to prevent landlords from evicting them for non-payment of rent. This tripped the alarm bell in the minds of the customer about the continuity of the project. Also, a few employees' visas were nearing expiry, and the service provider was reluctant to undertake its renewal as his earlier bills were still pending payment. Without an extension of the permit, employees would have to return to India.

When I met Peter Kaliaropoulos, CEO of Batelco, I could see he was sceptical about Satyam's ability to deliver. The project was behind by a few weeks, partly due to visa issues and partly due to other disruptions. When I persuaded Peter to allow us to continue, he was ruthless. 'Forget about it,' is what he said. I referred to the Indian government backing the revival, to which he responded, 'It doesn't matter.'

I was almost shown the door. I requested Peter to give me a slot for the next day, by which time I assured him I would sort things out. He reluctantly agreed.

I spoke to Hyderabad and advised them to immediately clear the visa agent's bills. On the way to the site, I talked to the agent to get us the visas and renewals without delay and told him our money would hit his bank account in the next few hours, clearing all arrears.

I met the on-site execution team. There were 30 men, all grim, gloomy and wearing a hangdog expression, concerned about rent, visas and salary. I told them about how we were working towards Satyam's revival.

At the meeting, an associate was curious to know the probability of his family joining him in Bahrain or the undesirable likelihood of returning to India due to either visa expiry or project default. I smiled. 'Don't worry. All will be well.' As he blinked, confused, I elaborated, 'Yes, we are in a difficult situation, but we are not here to succumb to setbacks but to surmount them. Our inner energy is superior to the bottlenecks we face. So, cheer up and give your best, and we will take care of the rest.'

I could see their faces light up with hope and faith.

As I got ready to leave, I told the anxious associates that on 23 January, while on his way to the hospital for bypass surgery, Prime Minister Manmohan Singh had enquired with the cabinet secretary about the progress of Satyam's revival plans. For the first time, I saw our team smile. I realized I had lightened their hearts and strengthened their resolve. The information Tarun gave us at the board meeting on 27 January had come in handy. I suddenly saw a spring in their step and a spark in their eyes.

Of course, I had a heavy heart as all their worries transmitted to me. This was normal. Having handled complex cases in tax matters involving 'search and seizure' for over a quarter century, I was accustomed to carrying clients' burdens until they were successfully settled.

The next day, when I met Peter, he was pleasantly surprised by the quick measures taken over the last 24 hours to clear operational issues. I suggested he could stagger the payments for the $3.5 million contract payments based on milestones achieved. To my relief, he was agreeable to the modified payment terms. I shook hands and we parted. Another client had been saved!

While in Bahrain, I monitored the salary payouts in the US, Europe and other parts of the world. To the surprise of the employees, Satyam honoured the salary for the month of January. I conveyed to my colleagues on the board the happy news of smooth disbursements and kept them posted on significant developments. In the first few board meetings, Deepak's secretary K.V. Viswanathan accompanied him, and we became good friends. Looking at the odd hours I sent emails, Viswanathan called to ask if I was getting adequate sleep and advised me to take care of my health. I was touched by his gesture.

After returning to India, I periodically monitored the honouring of commitments with both BMI and Batelco.

However, the story doesn't end there. In April 2009, while I was driving down M.G. Road in Bengaluru, my handset buzzed. I parked the vehicle in the service lane and took the call. I was moved when Peter congratulated me on Satyam's revival and apologized for hurting my sentiments in our first meeting. I thanked him and cheerfully said, 'I do not believe in love at first sight. I prefer to take a second look, and my memory of our second meeting is pleasant.'

I could feel the relief and happiness at the other end.

◆

This episode with Peter took my mind back to 1979.

As an articled trainee, I accompanied my senior, K. Venkata Subbiah Naidu, to Mumbai for tax assessments. The tax offices were scattered across the city. My principal, then 80 years old, fell sick and wanted me to meet the commissioner of income tax (Appeals) at his Parel office and seek an adjournment. Instead of carrying just an adjournment letter, I spent the night preparing for the case like a full-fledged professional!

I reached the commissioner's office on time and was called in. When I explained the situation to him, he was furious. 'Do you know how many times your senior has sought a date change? I am going to pass an adverse ex parte order.'

'Sir, I am well informed of the case, and if you permit, I can make the submissions.'

'Who are you?'

'I am an articled trainee with the firm, Sir.'

'What? You want me to hear out a trainee. Get out of my room.'

I came out and waited. An hour later, the commissioner stepped out to use the restroom. When he returned, I stood beside his door and smiled. After going in, he rang the bell and asked me to come in. 'Why have you not gone yet?'

'Sir, the client should not suffer, and my aged senior is unwell and unable to appear. If you can give me five minutes to recite the merits of the case, it would be helpful.'

He reluctantly opened the file and I explained ground after ground, narrating facts and citing relevant precedents. He heard me for over 45 minutes and asked a few questions, which I readily answered. He offered me a cup of tea at the end of it and wished me well for the exams.

A fortnight later, the client received a favourable order allowing the appeal in full.

The experience taught me an important lesson. In life, people may—due to circumstances, their stature or anxiety levels—belittle you. Do not take that to heart. Remember, you are there to achieve a purpose. Focus on the purpose irrespective of how badly you get treated.

◆

The company's fifth board meeting was held on 4 and 5 February, and Achuthan chaired it. By now, both IDBI and BoB had sanctioned short-term working capital loans to the tune of ₹300 crore each. The board passed the required resolutions to enable the creation of mortgages by a deposit of title deeds.

The BCG made a presentation. So did the forensic auditors, KPMG and Deloitte. While appreciating the progress made so far, we wanted the auditors to accelerate work by deploying an additional workforce.

We were still without a CEO. You cannot run a company as big as Satyam without filling this slot. We could fill it with a Satyam veteran or take someone from outside. BCG did an extensive in-house search and suggested A.S. Murthy, the company's head of Global Delivery and Leadership Development Programme, for the interim CEO position. After due process, the board decided to appoint Murthy as the company's CEO. It was an interim position because we believed that the new suitors might like to take an independent call.

Further, the board approved Homi Khusrokhan and Partho Datta's appointment as special advisors to assist in management and finance areas, respectively. Homi, a CA, had just retired as managing director of Tata Tea Limited and had once headed the multinational Glaxo. Partho, a CA, recently retired as group finance director of the House of Murugappa.

Homi began guiding Murthy. Since I was devoting my full time to Satyam and Partho was available to mentor the finance team, the board decided not to appoint a CFO. Both Homi and Partho visited Hyderabad each week for two or three days and were available every day on call. The two served Satyam pro bono and supported both the interim CEO and the board to define priorities and execute them effectively.

On the second day of the meeting, we had a couple of hours of discussion with SEC officials. They briefed us on the US's perspective and outlined their expectations from us. They requested cooperation with ongoing investigations and suggested we restate the financials with credible figures and disclosures in the next few months. In turn, we placed our concerns before them. We told the SEC about the extraordinary situation we were in. For the first time in Indian history, a government had intervened to protect investors', employees' and customers' interests. We explained the various measures taken, including the appointment of forensic auditors, internal auditors, legal advisors and special advisors. We told them we were nominated for a short duration until a strategic investor took over. We persuaded them not to target the company but instead focus on strengthening the oversight by regulators.

The SEC was on the same page as us and indicated that their interest was to send a proper signal to prevent the recurrence of such happenings. The board confirmed that the SEC contact would be Shardul Shroff in India and Lawrence Sucharow in the US.

In the press release issued after the meeting, Achuthan said, 'I am confident we are on the right track and we will be able to safeguard the interests of our customers, associates, investors and other stakeholders.'[1]

As usual, after the board meeting, I stayed back in Hyderabad.

On 6 February, I discussed the legal issues with corporate counsel K.B. Iyappa and his team. We took stock of all pending claims and were briefed on how they were being attended to. We decided litigation should be launched only if persuasion and arbitration failed. In the evening, we received the happy news that the MCA had appointed Kiran as chairman of the Satyam board.

I had a few overseas calls with customers and held discussions with the finance team to prepare the projected cash flow statement that could clear both statutory and non-statutory dues by March 2009.

---

[1] 'Press Release of Satyam Dated February 5, 2009', SEC, https://bit.ly/3aOT0V6. Accessed on 20 July 2022.

Meanwhile, the Indian Railways threatened to cancel our contract on enterprise resource planning (ERP) for the Loco Shed Management System and disqualify Satyam for the next 10 years unless a bank guarantee for ₹54 lakh was given. Our request to have the bank guarantee staggered did not find favour. We somehow managed to save the contract by bending to their terms.

The energy to smile sapped when we were asked by Bharat Sanchar Nigam Limited to obtain banker solvency!

As a board, we ensured that Satyam associates cooperated in the investigations by various agencies such as SFIO, Central Bureau of Investigation (CBI), SEBI, ED and RoC. We actively told them to cooperate. And since the finance team was working with me, we made sure that they were relieved from office work to go and appear before the investigating bodies. These agencies reciprocated by allowing the forensic auditors to gain access to the seized records.

Kiran, Deepak and Tarun were in regular touch with the ministry, and Achuthan and the legal advisors met SEBI regularly, and either Secretary Anurag Goel or Joint Secretary Jitesh Khosla would call me for occasional clarifications. Of course, through the periodical reports we submitted to the government, they were updated on Satyam's progress. So, on 7 February, when I told them the board is taking measures to trigger the process of identifying the strategic investor at the earliest, they heaved a sigh of relief.

In the week beginning 9 February, a month after Raju's letter, I had a series of meetings at Satyam's Mayfair office. I cleared the board minutes drafted by the company secretary. The finance team and I discussed issues relating to credit facilities with banks. We ensured Amex card dues were settled. There were conversations about the next US payroll payment. I had a word with Srinivasu Satti (Head, M&A) about the payments. V. Murali explained the Upaid case-related documentation.

Vijay Rangineni, COO, Satyam BPO, and I had a long chat on the business's future.

During one of those days, I noticed the CBI bring Ramalinga Raju to the visitors' area for questioning in the presence of a few associates. I sent word that they could use the conference room. The CBI politely refused. It was then that I saw Raju for the first and only time, and that too from a distance.

◆

Press Release, 5 February 2009

Satyam

Satyam Board names

Chief Executive Officer;
Special Advisors
&
Confirms receiving Loan sanctions

- Mr. A.S. Murty to assume CEO responsibilities
- Appoints Mr. Homi Khusrokhan and Mr. Partho Datta as Special Advisors to Board; Move aimed at strengthening management and financial areas

HYDERABAD, India, Feb. 05, 2009: Satyam Computer Services Limited (NYSE: SAY), a global consulting and information technology services provider, today said that its full Board met over two days (4th and 5th Feb 2009) along with their Advisors. This was the fifth meeting of the Board (in less than a month) and was chaired by Mr. Achuthan, former Presiding Officer of Securities Appellate Tribunal and Member of the Board.

The Board announced that it has appointed Mr. A.S. Murty as Satyam's Chief Executive Officer, effective immediately.

"Mr. Murty ('ASM') is a Satyam veteran of 15 years, who has been in its forefront since Jan 1994. He brings to play a deep understanding of the organization, proven expertise in leading a Business Unit, overseeing Global Delivery, nurturing Customer relationships and spearheading the entire gamut of the Human Resources function. He is well respected for his ability to effectively integrate the team and enable a collective decision making - which will be critical as Satyam moves into its revival phase." said Mr. Deepak Parekh, Member of the Board.

"In our interactions over the past few weeks, we are convinced that Satyam needs an internal leader to steer it at this critical juncture and ASM has the required bandwidth and support." added Mr. Parekh.

The Board also announced the appointment of Mr. Homi Khusrokhan and Mr. Partho Datta as Special Advisors to the Board, to assist in Management and Finance areas, respectively. The Special Advisors, along with Boston Consulting Group will work pro bono and will assist the newly named CEO and the Board, in defining priorities and executing them, effectively.

These decisions are aimed at quickly stabilizing Satyam. The organization has visibly increased its focus on business continuity for its customers and confidence building amongst its associates (employees) and vendors.

"This is a unique opportunity to provide direction and guidance and I accept it with all humility. I have no misgivings about the enormity of the task in front of us, but together with my colleagues, I am confident we can accomplish the impossible. I look forward to working very closely with the Board, our Advisors and all Satyamites – to restore Satyam to its well-deserved glory. We will chart a precise and practical 30 – 60 – 90 day plan that will encompass and address the interests of all stakeholders." Mr. Murty said

Commented Mr. Khusrokhan on his role : "Having led large organizations before, I expect this opportunity to be a singularly enriching experience and I look forward to contributing my might to this noble task".

Referring to another significant development, the board today confirmed receiving bank sanctions for a total sum of Rs. 600 Crores (USD 130 Mn. approx) as a planned fund infusion towards working capital requirements. This funding, along with healthy collections, is expected to help the company tide over its financial challenges. Satyam also reaffirmed that January 09 salaries (globally) and the fortnightly salary in Feb 09 (for its US based associates) have been met from its internal accruals. (US payroll is run fortnightly for US based associates and has been so since company's inception).

"Completing the complex financial restatement exercise including announcement of Q3 results and ensuring prudent financial operations will be the primary focus in the next few weeks" Mr Datta added. He will be overseeing the financial operations of the company

NAVIGATING THROUGH TURBULENCE

The Board confirmed that their key priorities and collective focus remain unchanged:

- Reaching out to key Customers & associates to reinforce their trust and confidence
- Asserting the financial position and restatement of Q3 results
- Evaluating long-term strategic options, in consultation with the Advisors
- Assessing legal liabilities and dealing with them comprehensively
- Undertaking cost rationalization measures
- Resuming investments in identified areas

Wachtell, Lipton, Rosen & Katz (www.wlrk.com) have been appointed as Satyam's lawyers to address the Class Action suits in US. Latham & Watkins have been lawyers to Satyam for over eight years and they will continue to support Satyam in its continuing dialogue with US SEC.

"I am confident that we are on the right track and we will be able to safeguard interests of our customers, associates, investors and other stakeholders" said Mr. Achuthan, Member of the Board, who chaired today's meeting.

9
SATYAM'S SWOT

In my first week at the job, I studied various aspects of Satyam to understand how the 21-year-old company worked. It led to me drawing a 20-point SWOT (Strengths, Weaknesses, Opportunities and Threats) analysis and identifying a minimum of four strategies. These are what I scribbled on separate sheets of white paper in my handwriting.

Later, as we moved along the road to recovery, we implemented some of these measures. We handed over the 'work-in-progress' to the new owners for completion. A few actions, which were only at the drawing board stage, were also shared with them for implementation.

STRENGTHS

World-class infrastructure

Satyam owned properties in Hyderabad, Bengaluru, Vizag and Pune, and those accommodated Software Technology Park (STP) and Special Economic Zone (SEZ) units.[1] It had

---

[1] The STP is a scheme of the Government of India meant to encourage development and export of computer software. In contrast, an SEZ is a cordoned area that is governed by special business and trade laws to encourage additional economic activity, promote exports, attract domestic and foreign investments, create employment opportunities and develop infrastructure facilities.

similar STP and SEZ campuses in Bhubaneswar, Chennai, Kolkata and Nagpur on 99 years' lease. Besides, there were locations developed on leased land abroad—in Malaysia, China and Australia. Also, Satyam had 31 global solution centres and regular leased premises housing offices spread across India as well as globally.

Two prime campuses of the company were in Hyderabad. The first was in Madhapur in Hi-Tech City, spread over 19.72 acres of land. You must walk into the Madhapur campus to experience its elegance first-hand. This was where all our Hyderabad board meetings were held.

The second was the breathtaking Satyam Technology Center (STC), Bahadurpally, built across 118 acres. It was surrounded on the north and east by reserve forest and combined state-of-the-art infrastructure with a close-to-nature setting. A new SEZ unit was also under construction.

Peeping through the office window, you could see a golf course, a deer park and an aviary that housed exotic birds. A large part of the campus was a forest area. Here, you would find trees and flower plants growing everywhere and birds flying around. This proximity to nature helped create a harmonious, productive environment and added a fantastic dimension to business and leisure activities.

Both campuses had auditoriums with excellent acoustics. Besides, there were training halls and meeting rooms. The place was home to health clubs and swimming pools. Battery-operated cars transported people within the campus. Satyam had got well-equipped classrooms and labs in all its locations with an overall training capacity of over 2,000 seats for instructor-led learning. The STC alone accommodated 1,500 people in a single shift. There was a perfect amphitheatre as well.

It was a spectacular real estate property.

Excellent talent pool

Satyam had 17 subsidiaries globally. The company began in 1987 with 20 people, grew slowly, soon picked momentum and then raced to over 51,000 employees by December 2008, comprising 60 nationalities![2] HR took care of recruiting, training and nurturing talent in various segments of the industry.

A well-qualified and experienced management team, supported by executive talent at the ground level, helped provide a broad spectrum of services, including end-to-end manufacturing services. In some verticals such as banking and financial services, insurance, telecom, retail, manufacturing and automotive divisions, Satyam had star associates trained to compete with the world's best.

The company's senior associates had enormous loyalty towards Satyam in an era when job-hopping was second nature. A few of them had been with the company since the early 1990s. They were well paid and respected. I learnt that during the crisis, NASSCOM discreetly sent out a message to the software industry not to poach Satyam's top brass. I must say to their everlasting credit, the companies heeded it.

Satyam leaders got some excellent non-monetary benefits like membership to the Full Life Cycle Leadership initiative, the Satyam School of Leadership (SSL) and the Satyam Learning Center (SLC). The first mentioned provided employees with early leadership opportunities and job rotations, which enabled them to move across various technologies, domains and geographies.

Both the SLC and SSL trained employees to take up higher responsibilities. The former conducted regular workshops and seminars in technical and soft skills to upgrade the knowledge base of associates. Facilities included computer laboratories,

---

[2]Ghosh, Debasmita, 'Satyam Computers to Axe 4,500 Employees', *The Economic Times*, 15 September 2008, https://bit.ly/3J6UbMj. Accessed on 25 July 2022.

classrooms, video- and computer-based learning tools, and an extensive library. Apart from very competent internal faculty members, SLC used eminent specialists and academics to deliver training courses. SSL was established by Satyam to groom senior associates into becoming tomorrow's business leaders. The idea was to identify potential leaders from Satyam's senior associate base, enhance leadership skills through holistic learning interventions and nurture them to manage wholesome responsibilities.

Satyam created a pool of human resources with leadership traits that bonded with affinity. They wouldn't cross over either for the excitement of a new job or for the money because the Rajus historically treated them with dignity and respect.

The brilliant talent pool was a very significant intangible asset.

Premium customers

Satyam was doing business with over 650 customers, of whom 185 were among the Fortune 500 companies. The spread of services offered included application development and maintenance, consulting and enterprise solutions, and business intelligence. There were enterprise applications, SAP and testing, and industry-native solutions. They had integrated engineering services, infrastructure services, emergency and healthcare management, market research, and customer analytics to top it. Name it, and Satyam had it.

The dominant sectors were healthcare, manufacturing, automotive, telecom, infrastructure, media, entertainment, energy and utilities.

When 95 per cent of the sale is export, it says something good about how the business has been world class. North America alone contributed 60 per cent. Together, Europe (21 per cent) and the Asia Pacific (14 per cent) accounted for 35 per cent, whereas India contributed a tiny 3 per cent and the

Rest of the World 2 per cent. Satyam was indeed a company catering only to global players.[3]

Low borrowings

As of the date of the confession, the level of borrowings from banks was not significant. The funded borrowings, the non-fund-based facilities and foreign exchange exposure in aggregate were about ₹750 crore. Considering the magnitude of operations, Satyam could take additional financial exposure to survive during these critical times. Yes, it had room for leverage in its capital structure.

The good news was that barring the fictitious sum Raju had indicated in his confession, the rest on the debtors' list was good. We at least knew money was somewhere available to tap! We could create an additional charge on receivables if needed. And if push came to shove, we could offer bankers real estate property on an equitable mortgage, as they were unencumbered.

WEAKNESSES

Tainted image

At the board, we understood the need to retain existing clients and win new ones. A few customers were migrating, and we had to plug the hole; else, the ship would sink. We knew the recent wins would compensate for the big names that were leaving us. It would also boost the marketing team's confidence, send out a signal to the outside world and stop the further exodus.

However, we faced a stumbling block—the 'taint' associated with Satyam. Everywhere we turned, the prefix 'scam-hit', 'fraud-hit' or 'scam-tainted' stared right at us. 'Satyam', which in several Indian languages meant 'truth', was getting the opposite

---

[3] 21st Annual Report, Satyam, FY 2007–08, p. 59.

image. The brand of Satyam was so tarnished, we found it challenging to bag new orders. If we still managed, it was due to a fortuitous combination of a fabulous talent pool, our persistent efforts and providence, viz., an Act of God.

Huge operational costs

In the financial year 2007–08, the rate at which operational costs had increased had been faster than the rate at which revenue had grown. Hence, margins were subdued.

Due to high operational costs, the actual profit was 3 per cent of turnover against the industry norm of about 10–20 per cent. Thanks to creative accounting, Satyam projected a higher margin during several quarters and an exceptionally healthy 24 per cent in the last two quarters, viz., June 2008 and September 2008.

Raju confirmed much of these in his confession.

With Murthy in the forefront as the CEO, we implemented a few cost-reduction measures. For instance, on non-billable travel, we made people do video-conferencing, which was catching fancy in the wake of the global financial crisis. Physical journey was only on an absolutely must basis. There was also enough room for saving costs for board and lodging by encouraging overnight trips and entering into tie-ups for a discounted tariff.

Lack of controls and processes

For any organization, and more so a listed entity, you must put adequate controls and processes to ensure the financial figures reported are reliable. It is based on the financial statements that stakeholders such as investors, lenders, customers, regulators and government departments take decisions. Unless you have a robust process, manipulations and fudging can happen. There was human intervention in exporting and importing data from verticals to the finance team in Satyam, which should be unacceptable for a tech company. This was perhaps deliberately kept, allowing for playing around with the data, as fudging would not have been possible with automation. The best process for financial data is to introduce automation with an ERP system for seamless migration to protect the data's authenticity. Alas, there was no foolproof mechanism for data integration with appropriate checks and balances. Manual intervention was permissible.

I was given to understand different codes were used even in the system. The 'H' code would show the actual figures by hiding fictitious data, and the 'S' code would show the statistics, including the fictitious data. Of course, these codes were known only to a select few, and only they knew 'H' means HIDE, and 'S' implies SHOW!

Cash flow

While the debtors' figure in the books was genuine, we expected difficulty in collections. Money collected from customers was the oxygen that kept Satyam breathing. The last thing we wanted was an employee walking away because we could not pay. Remember, customers could stagger payments, and we could ill-afford to take chances. If there was a mismatch in the cash inflow and outflow, defaults might lead to tricky consequences.

On the one hand, while statutory arrears were causing stress, the other overdue to service providers and vendors could stop the flow of goods and services. If we didn't honour commitments to agents rendering visa services globally, it might derail our ability to deploy employees and upset the project delivery schedule. The cash reserve of ₹600 crore for meeting at least one month's operational need representing ₹500 crore for salaries and ₹100 crore for administration costs, independent of customers' collections, was necessary to prevent a liquidity crisis. This was why we sought bank financing to the extent of ₹600 crore.

OPPORTUNITIES

Unencumbered assets

The existing borrowings were against receivables. When Satyam borrowed, it offered these receivables as collateral security. It meant that in the event of default by Satyam, the bank could instruct the customer to directly pay the bank. The other assets were free of charge. We could pledge our two campuses, valued at ₹1,700 crore, to raise new loan facilities from IDBI and BoB. True, bankers weren't bending backwards to lend to Satyam, but there were many, particularly in the public sector, that felt duty-bound to save the company and chipped in with help. Deepak's presence on the board was a big help in this direction as well as the fact that we had unencumbered assets, which we could mortgage.

Support from the government, CLB and SEBI

The government offered unconditional support. Both the MCA and SEBI, not to speak of the Company Law Tribunal, gave the board immense strength to make appropriate and timely shifts, and carry out an action plan without legal hassles.

On 31 March 2009, the government even clarified that Satyam, under the new board, may be regarded as a government company for specific purposes. The relaxation and approvals on every petition moved before them were quick and favourable; it helped us execute the revival with ease. But the government never intervened in any of our strategies or their execution. We were given 100 per cent freedom and independence in making decisions. Some of the people who were especially helpful and supportive were: T.K.A. Nair, principal secretary to the prime minister; K.M. Chandrasekhar, cabinet secretary; Anurag Goel, secretary, MCA; and Jitesh Khosla, joint secretary, MCA.

Once the MCA wrote to the chairman of the Railway Board, saying,

> In view of the efforts being made by the government and the new board to put the company back on its feet, it is urged that requirements based on audited financial statements may be dispensed with, and the bid of the company considered on technical proficiency, price, and financial information provided by its current board. In fact, benefits/concessions normally available to government companies may also be extended to Satyam as long as it is under the management of government-appointed directors. This would not only provide a reasonable playing field to Satyam but also go a long way in restoring the faith of the stakeholders of the company worldwide in the strategy adopted by the government and the new board to deal with the current crisis confronting the company.[4]

Government-nominated board

The board had men with rich experience in corporate India and in jurisprudence. Deepak Parekh had built HDFC brick-by-brick. As president of NASSCOM, Kiran Karnik gave a facelift to the outsourcing industry's credibility and was the czar of networking. Tarun Das, a chief mentor of the CII, was aware of making companies work in the most adverse situations.

Then, we had C. Achuthan, the man who knew capital market jurisprudence inside out. The presence of S. Balakrishna Mainak representing LIC, a shareholder in Satyam, sent a positive signal to shareholders. My being a former president of the ICAI and my ability to devote full time to execute the board's strategy and operating decisions showed we meant business.

This belief in our dedication was conveyed to me by a

---
[4]Letter of the MCA dated 31 March 2009.

former student. Her mother was on a visit to the US to spend time with her son. In the condominium they lived, a few Satyam employees stayed. In a social gathering at the club house, the Satyamites were discussing their bleak future and the high probability of their not getting January 2009 salaries. The lady, having overheard the conversation, got herself introduced to them. She went up to the group and said, 'I know Manoharan. Now that he is on the Satyam board, you can be assured your salaries will be paid.'

I was touched by the confidence she reposed in me. I told myself, 'If not for anything else, at least for this faith, which people have in me, I must go the extra mile in ensuring a positive outcome.'

Not easy to move out

In the manufacturing industry, you can replace a supplier within 24 hours. In the software industry, it is not so easy. There is a gestation period needed to build a new relationship and migrate to the new service provider. If there aren't enough people with the requisite domain expertise among the competitors, it could still be harder.

This gave us lead time to both show and tell our clients that we were as good as before, if not better. We could persuade our customers to hold on before terminating. In the interregnum, we showed them the crisis was internal and would not impact either the project execution or service delivery. That is how customer attrition stopped beyond a point.

THREATS

Investigating agencies

First, the CB-CID, and two months later, the CBI carried out investigations into Satyam's affairs. Various agencies under different laws such as SFIO, ED, Economic Offences Wing, SEC and SEBI initiated inquiries to probe into matters falling under their jurisdiction. Of course, these agencies were just doing their job. However, from a Satyam employee's perspective, particularly the finance and treasury team, much time was taken away in being summoned and interrogated. Likewise, many of the top leaders were called for interrogation. All this was demoralizing for the associates.

However, I must concede that after some time, the agencies understood our predicament and carried out the investigation without hindering the revival process. The associates also cooperated. The relationship was cordial, and we supplemented each other's efforts.

Vasagiri Venkata Lakshminarayana was the CBI-DIG (Deputy Inspector General of Police). The IIT-IPS officer headed the 15-member multidisciplinary investigation team. Honest and upright, he was professional in his approach. He quietly segregated those who committed the fraud from those who carried out their duties, unaware of the crime. Therefore, the arrests were confined to only eight people other than the Raju brothers.[5] All innocent souls must be forever grateful to Lakshminarayana.

The media

The most challenging part of those 100 days was handling the media. The press was hungry for bits of news that could be sensationalized. Chairman Karnik was flooded with calls on estimates, predictions, and the like. Often, he refused. The press had links in various quarters and, at times, surprised us with an accurate reporting on confidential matters.

---

[5] 'Satyam Verdict Announced: All You Need to Know About the Satyam Fraud Case', *India Today*, 11 April 2015, https://bit.ly/3ORbjHf. Accessed on 1 August 2022.

In the initial days, several rumours were floating as headlines in the media, causing anxiety for the associates. Satyam's communications team sent out a daily bulletin to all its associates, listing every such rumour and giving Satyam's version. This clarified the issue and restored associates' confidence in the company.

We thought negative coverage by the media and their positions could cause discomfort in stakeholders' minds. Often, the press reports a problem but not the solution, because it is never considered newsworthy. However, I must add that due to the board's friendly approach, the media was very supportive during the revival's final days. The several positive stories they published helped Satyam to be in the reckoning among the ultimate bidders.

Government departments

Even as a government-nominated board, we faced challenges from some of the government departments. The Income Tax Department had frozen Satyam's bank accounts. Similar demands from the commercial taxes department and PF authorities were faced. It was like strangulating the already cash-starved company. Provisional orders by the Income Tax Department for attaching Satyam's properties created bottlenecks in raising money from banks. Of course, the government machinery had to do its work, but it diverted our precious effort from the crucial task of revival.

Bankers

Much time was spent in negotiating with banks, especially the foreign banks, for extension of existing facilities and renegotiating the terms of repayment and security. While we understood their concerns, the bankers were too rigid with their conditions. Matters like appropriating collections against dues to them, while legal, went against the revival spirit we were fighting so hard to establish. Star bankers, who once knocked on Satyam's doors to lend, were now avoiding any association with the company.

Tender requirements for new orders

When we bid for new orders, we hit a wall. The tenders required us to furnish audited financial statements for the previous three years (2005–06, 2006–07 and 2007–08). How were we to do so when the world knew our numbers were suspect? We also had to provide bank guarantees for bidding and performance, but the bankers wanted a 100 per cent margin in some cases and 110 per cent in others. The extra 10 per cent was to meet incidental expenses if they had to encash the guarantees! I would later learn that it also factored 'a premium for dealing with a "tainted" company'!

We could do it in case of some. New Mangalore Port Trust wanted a confirmation from the auditors that the company's annual turnover was more than ₹10 crore and that the net financial worth was at least ₹100 crore in each of the last three financial years. Similarly, the Railways wanted a confirmation that the turnover was more than ₹200 crore for three select financial years.

A few tenders asked the company to attach a solvency certificate! A solvency certificate confirms that the company has a positive net worth and that the realizable value of its assets is more than the payable value of its liabilities. This certificate is required by the government and commercial offices to be sure about the financial position of individuals or entities. In the situation we were in, which banker or professional would certify? Despite all these hassles, Satyam did secure specific orders—some renewals and some brand new—and every such instance gave impetus to the revival process.

Recession in the IT industry

The global financial crisis that originated in the US and Europe in 2008 had its gradual impact on the rest of the world and, in particular, in developing economies like India. The booming IT industry faced a slowdown due to a decline in orders from the West. While the recession exposed the Satyam scam, the same recession helped us retain the associates since they found it difficult to take chances during a slowdown!

Third-party claims

Thirty-seven Hyderabad-based agro companies wrote to Satyam asking for confirmation of loan amounts given by them to Satyam. The total amount was ₹1,230 crore and matched with the sum indicated by Raju in his confession. There was no board resolution authorizing such borrowing. Forensic auditors also did not find their names in the books. The matter is sub judice till date.

There were some claims about Satyam's recent acquisitions and settlement of the terms pending closure. Furthermore, Upaid Systems Limited, incorporated in the British Virgin Islands, demanded $100 million towards infringement of rights and allegations of forgery, etc., by Satyam.[6] Several vultures were flying in, scenting the carcass!

Class-action suits in the US

About 12 suits were filed in New York courts by groups of shareholders. They claimed damages from Satyam for the erosion of their wealth due to a drop in stock prices. They attributed the fall to the falsification of financial statements. These cases were widely publicized in the media and dented Satyam's reputation in the minds of the customers. We engaged

---

[6]'Satyam Offers $10 Mn to Settle Upaid's $1 Bn Claim', *Mint*, 10 May 2009, https://bit.ly/3B0w2U8, accessed on 12 September 2022.

legal advisors both in India and the US to handle the issues. We asked the US lawyers to defend Satyam in class-action suits and in matters of compliance with SEC requirements.

A delegation from SEC visited India twice. The first time was on 5 February 2009 and the second time on 14 July 2009. During these visits, they met the investigating agencies besides meeting SEBI, the legal advisors and the Satyam board. The trip was to get into an understanding of the mutual exchange of information and follow-up action. As chairman of the audit committee, I had an hour-long discussion with them on 14 July, and we exchanged updates. The SEC felt reassured that India fully understood the investigative measures. Therefore, it decided not to step in and duplicate the effort.

◆

SATYAM 'SWOT'

STRENGTHS (S)	WEAKNESSES (W)
1. World-class infrastructure 2. Excellent talent pool 3. Premium customers 4. Low borrowings	1. Tainted image 2. Huge operational costs 3. Lack of controls and processes 4. Cash flow
OPPORTUNITIES (O)	**THREATS (T)**
1. Unencumbered assets 2. Support from the government, CLB and SEBI 3. Government-nominated board 4. Not easy to move out	1. Investigating agencies 2. The media 3. Government departments 4. Bankers 5. Tender requirements for new orders 6. Recession in the IT industry 7. Third-party claims 8. Class-action suits in the US

From the SWOT, we did draw up strategies and action plans.

STRATEGIES ADOPTED

1. Use unencumbered assets (O1) to raise money (W4);
2. Use government, CLB and regulators' support (O2) to obtain relaxations and exemptions from a few regulatory and legal hurdles and to reschedule statutory payments (T3);
3. Use talent pool to deliver quality service (S2) to gain lead time (O4) and remove taint (W1);
4. Use recession (T6) to implement cost reduction (W2) and retain associates.

PART 5

HOW WE DID IT

10

REJUVENATING EMPLOYEES

As board members, our top three priorities were (a) restoring financial stability, (b) motivating employees, and (c) retaining customers. Although the three were tied together, with one leading to the other, we had to attend to them in parallel.

In a service organization like Satyam, people are the most critical asset. N.R. Narayana Murthy, a doyen of the IT industry, once famously said, 'Our core corporate assets walk out every evening, mentally and physically tired. It is our duty to make sure that these assets return well rested, energetic and enthusiastic the next morning.'[1] If it is valid for a bellwether company, imagine what it would be like for Satyam, a company surviving on borrowed time.

To take a marine analogy, employees are the crew, while the customers are the passengers on a ship called Satyam. In the engulfing storm, we badly needed the crew to not jump ship. So, as captains, we had to keep them motivated somehow. God forbid, if we failed, the crisis would spiral, and it would become difficult to hold back the passengers, namely the customers. But if employees delivered work on time and didn't compromise on quality, customers would stay with us. If customers remained, financial stability would follow. We had no other way of gaining financial stability to win corporate India's most prominent war,

---

[1]Majumdar, Shyamal, 'Meaningful Engagement', *Business Standard*, 20 January 2013, https://bit.ly/3PyYhPZ. Accessed on 26 July 2022.

as the government had minced no words in telling us they would not loosen the purse strings. What a loop!

MOTIVATING THE ASSOCIATES

When we joined Satyam, we realized we needed to bond with the leadership and employees to complete our mission. However, what we saw on the ground were abysmally low morale and a sense of doom. With this mindset, you cannot bond much. But we understood the associates' sentiment.

If you are used to a particular lifestyle, you get shaken up when some of the comforts associated with that lifestyle are removed. Imagine you, who travel by car, have to take a bus now. Imagine you, who used to dine in restaurants once a week, have to think twice before going out once a month. Associates found themselves in a similar situation after their former boss Raju's confession letter. It hurt them financially as well as emotionally. Yes, the Satyam employees, all honourable men and women, were down in the dumps, demoralized. These people, who wore their Satyam badge with pride for years together, now hid it under their dress. They no longer walked with their chin up. Society had started to look down upon them, even when they were not a party to the fraud. And when confidence takes such a beating, depression sets in.

Added to all this was their private wealth. Many employees had parked their entire savings in employee stock option plans (ESOPs) at a market price ranging from ₹200 to ₹300 per share in many cases, and at a higher price in some cases. Suddenly, they found the share price had hit ₹8 and was hovering around ₹20. Stocks and shares became shocks and stares. While no official statement had been put up about firing or downsizing, job security became an issue. The prospects of getting the following month's salary appeared bleak. For the first time, employees realized what it was to hold onto a job. The fear was real and palpable.

The arrest of the chairman, the managing director, the CFO, a few members of the accounts team and the statutory auditors shook both the top management and team leaders. Remember, Raju was a shining star in society. PW was a global firm, and India did not have any history of arresting auditors over audit failure. Further, multiple investigative agencies were interrogating Satyam's business leaders and the executives in the finance and corporate services functions. The stress took its toll. We found it challenging to get things done by them after they returned from these soul-draining sessions. While the experience may not have been like what you see in movies, it was definitely not pleasant. They apprehended the needle of suspicion was directed at them. We often told them, 'If you have done no wrong, there is no need to worry.'

None of this was a recipe for happiness. So, in short, when we came in, employee motivation levels were at an all-time low.

◆

For us, on the board, there was no time to lose.

We realized we could turn around the company only with the active involvement and support of the associates. We reached out to every one of them to instill the belief that Satyam would be revived. We urged them to stay positive and focus on the mission of resurrecting the company.

Marketing and Communications Head T. Hari and HR Head S.V. Krishnan did everything possible to pass on the message that the government-nominated team was there to protect associates', customers' and investors' interests and thereby restore the company's pride. Whenever newspapers reported a setback in revival or published any negative news, the associates panicked. We quickly convinced them that things are not as bad as they were made out to be, and several positive happenings were not being reported either due to confidentiality or because they were not sensational enough.

Each week, team leaders across the globe connected to our headquarters, and some of us joined the call to communicate essential matters for dissemination among respective verticals. In some leadership calls, we pushed the leaders to pitch for new projects. We asked, 'Why should you be defensive when you have done no wrong?' We told them to get their marketing team to aggressively bid for new projects and spread the message that Satyam was back in business as usual. It worked. We bagged additional jobs from existing customers and won few new customers as well.

Gradually, these initiatives began to show results, and this cheered up the associates. And this positivity had a contagious effect.

Through Hari, ably supported by Indraneel Ganguly, we opened several communication channels to reach the associates. After Murthy took over as CEO, he reached out to the associates from his end as well. Given his wide acceptability in the organization, he could unite and inspire them. Hari and Indraneel were vibrant and creative in this endeavour to stay connected with the associates.

Every evening, we sent out an electronic news bulletin to all associates under the title 'News Today'. In it, we shared positive news about happenings in the company and about the revival steps we had taken.

As part of the 'Direct from the Leadership' campaign, business leaders gave their team pep talks each day, infusing confidence into them and encouraging them to put extra effort during these difficult times.

Next, we, the six directors, video recorded our message, and it was played at various locations worldwide and posted on YouTube. The associates knew Deepak Parekh as an institution builder. They knew Kiran Karnik as once the face of the software industry. To back the duo was Tarun Das, with friends in industry and government. These were all reassuring faces. My experience in delivering peppy motivational talks came in handy as well.

An initiative named 'Surf the Board' was started to help associates know what was happening in the company. These short bytes of board members were spread through the Intranet (Satyam World) and News Cast (News Today Live), and subsequently, uploaded on YouTube. The feedback was encouraging. Satyam leaders T.R. Anand, Shyam Sharma, Sandeep Sharma and Virender Aggarwal gushed in with tributes. So did Sanjukta Kulkarni and Alpna Doshi, in echoing the sentiments of the womenfolk. In addition, 24/7 help desk services were established to clarify queries, floor meetings and learning interventions were arranged, and counselling was initiated at project locations where the attrition rate was high.

'Breaking News' was a campaign to instantly flash positive news to associates. The idea was to convey the story as it happened and spread it faster than external sources. That way, associates would know we were on top of things and feel they were kept in the loop.

I knew this was a mind game and not about coding talent or skill. You don't lose your skills overnight merely because you feel betrayed by the man you looked up to. But you can lose your mind, morale and motivation in 24 hours flat. It was essential not to let that happen. The employees' skill set was still intact; they only needed to be supported emotionally. I interacted with vertical heads and group heads with this thought uppermost in my mind.

As I hopped from one meeting to another, one location to another, one geography to another, and one country to another, to meet and address the associates, I told them, 'We, the government-nominated directors, are strangers to your company. But you are all part of it. Many of you have grown with Satyam. You are what you are because of Satyam. This is the moment it needs you desperately. Please don't let the company down for whatever reason. Just put aside all the negativity in your mind, roll up your sleeves and resolve to give your best.

'I am now a part of Satyam and one among you. We, the board, are with you in this task to bring the company on track. Join hands with us in the revival, and we can turn Satyam around soon. After that, you can look back with a sense of satisfaction that you did the right thing in staying with the company when it mattered the most.'

It resonated well with them. Their hitherto gloomy faces transformed into smiling ones, full of hope. That momentum continued and in my future interactions, I could see them charged up to give it their best. The number of associates as on 31 March 2009 was 41,267 against 45,969 a year earlier. This fall by 10.2 per cent compares favourably with the IT industry's attrition rate of 15 per cent in 2009.[2]

The directors interacted with the media and this broadcast confidence. Deepak Parekh's interview with business journalist Omkar Goswami on NDTV PROFIT, Tarun Das engaging with television commentator Karan Thapar on CNBC and Kiran Karnik talking to TV anchor Shereen Bhan on CNBC-TV18 built confidence among associates and customers. It told them, if they needed to be told, that the board was fighting from the front.[3]

Slowly, it became clear that our energy levels and positive attitude were beginning to rub off on the leaders and from them down to the last associate. After we launched the 'Surf

---

[2]'IT 2008–09: Salary Hikes & Attrition', *The Times of India*, 21 September 2009, https://bit.ly/3zMH009. Accessed on 1 August 2022.
[3]'Question Time with Deepak Parekh', NDTV Profit, 19 February 2009, https://bit.ly/3zKLzrQ. Accessed on 1 August 2009.

the Board' campaign, daily queries dropped from 60 a day to less than five. Once we initiated the 'Direct from the Leadership' programme, it fell to zero, and then on associates focussed on delivery, knowing the company was in safe hands.

We always knew Satyam had some exciting talent working for it. Soon, an external proof came when an independent agency found we had outstanding leaders in a few verticals. We played up this information both with clients and with the associates. Every small win needed celebration.

◆

At times, we heard someone was planning to resign. If we felt we should retain them, one of us spoke to them, persuading the associate to rethink their decision. The approach made a difference, and we could see most people sticking with Satyam.

Deepak Nangia, head of Australia and New Zealand, wanted to leave. He was critical of our plans in the region. So, I called him to better understand his concerns. Apparently, he was frustrated with the developments and wanted to move on in life. I told him Satyam would soon be revived, and when that happened, we did not want him to miss the celebrations. I requested Nangia to sleep over the conversation. It worked! The next day, he called and said he would remain. He wanted to look back after revival with a sense of satisfaction that he had not jumped a sinking ship but anchored it to safety.

I planned for small celebrations. When bankers sanctioned a new facility or renewed an existing one, we didn't go to the bank to sign, nor did we sign in my room. We gathered every team member from finance, treasury, legal and corporate services in the conference hall, signed in their presence and celebrated the occasion. Only champagne was missing! Such small events boosted our morale.

I gave short speeches complimenting everybody and radiating a sense of accomplishment. I visited all the offices of Satyam in Hyderabad, Chennai and Bengaluru to address its associates. Some of them were physically present, while many joined via the internet from locations across the globe. I allowed unlimited time for their questions and had a free and frank conversation. During the informal interactions that followed my address, several associates freely shared their emotions. It deeply touched me.

They told me how the crisis impacted each one of them differently. In some cases, neighbours stopped talking to them. At social functions, acquaintances neither smiled nor shook hands. Restaurants who were once happy to grant attractive discounts to any associate walking in with family or friends were not so keen to receive them any more. These were the ground realities of the Satyam brand losing its mojo overnight.

We, the board members, were available to team leaders and associates round the clock. Similarly, they were always at our disposal to execute our many ideas. I spent several sleepless nights resolving issues. There were days when I cracked four out of the 10 points on hand and retired to bed with satisfaction, only to find I was engulfed with six new ones when I woke up. My most significant source of energy was the associates who fought against all odds. It was then that I experienced the true meaning of the saying, 'Our greatest glory is not in never falling down but in rising every time we fall.'

◆

In 2009, Gartner paid Satyam immeasurable encomiums when it wrote, 'Early reports directly from Satyam clients (especially those using more than 100 Satyam full-time equivalents) indicate that they have not experienced disruption or degradation of service. This is a testament to the resilience of Satyam employees.'

In Chennai, associates went ballistic with phrases like 'winners are not quitters'. One of them said, 'They never give up...they try and try to achieve. It makes me very proud that I am part of the company that is driven by leaders like you. We assure you that we all are and we will be standing behind Satyam Leadership at this moment.'

While many people compliment the government, the board, the customers and the regulators for Satyam's magical revival, I feel they miss one contingent. I believe the most generous contribution to getting Satyam back on track came from the associates. To use a phrase from the army, the associates stayed back like foot soldiers to fight the war. Without them, the generals could have done nothing.

FEEDBACK ON 'SURF THE BOARD'

T.R. Anand wrote, 'The commitment and passion shown by the board members are like a shining beacon for us.'

Sanjukta Kulkarni mailed, 'I just wanted to send a quick email to commend this initiative. We are delighted to have directors of this calibre, working hard towards getting us back on track.'

'This is awesome! Thoughts from Deepak Parekh and T.N. Manoharan are really inspiring. I am really thankful to have an eminent and responsible leadership, driving us through these times of crisis,' exclaimed Shyam Sharma.

'What an inspiring message. Feel totally indebted to these people who are helping us out in totally immeasurable ways,' said Alpna Doshi.

'So far, we had been getting a lot of communication from the leaders, but the board seemed to be in a different realm. It is nice to see T.N. Manoharan saying that he is part of Satyam now,' wrote Sandeep Sharma.

'The sincerity, openness and desire of our eminent board members to understand the details of our issues and resolve them quickly is remarkable,' commented Virender Aggarwal.

11

SYNERGY WITH CUSTOMERS

On another front, we kept talking with customers.

We didn't hide, sulk or succumb to shame. We stood to tell the world that Satyam was as much a victim of fraud as others. The board was there to segregate the good from the bad and protect and retain the good. In the end, this helped us win.

Some customers called on the board members at Hyderabad to get a feel of what was happening. Notable among them were National Australia Bank (NAB), CISCO Systems, GSK, General Electric, Coca-Cola, Scotiabank, Bombardier and Abercrombie & Fitch. Many of them and others were briefed over conference calls with scheduled fortnightly follow-up conversations. Between Kiran and me, we handled these matters.

There were days when my schedule was packed with customers, bankers and the leadership team. Work would start early, time would fly and the chef at the guesthouse would be disappointed at my having skipped the artfully cooked breakfast. Some days, I missed lunch and went straight for dinner. I know these were not healthy, but I was in mission mode. That is when one of the executives commented, 'The government has not put you on the hot seat; they have put you on the fire.' I smiled and said, 'Like hard metals, my melting point is beyond the heat this fire can generate!' Both of us had a hearty laugh.

As I look back with the advantage of hindsight, I think four factors influenced most of our customers to stay back.

One, Satyam had a great talent pool with a history of delivering high-quality service to customers. This helped us talk to customers with courage and conviction. We persuaded clients to give us some time and did follow-up calls to update them periodically. After answering their queries in every follow-up call, we asked how satisfied they were with the project's execution. Most of them said, 'While the quality of delivery was up to the mark before 7 January, it improved phenomenally after the confession!' This feedback energized us.

The second factor was they couldn't believe the government-nominated board, consisting of outstanding achievers in their respective spheres, was spending its time without drawing any monetary reward. It was unheard of anywhere in the world and truly inspired them. One stupefied CEO said, 'Incredible Indians.' After that, they gave a lot of weight to what we said and listened to us with the utmost respect. After all, the board was doing a transformational, and not a transactional, job.

The third factor that weighed in our favour was our being candid in our assurances. We said, 'Give us a few weeks and then evaluate us.' We asked them to judge us by our work. 'If the work is going right and you are comfortable continuing with Satyam, we would be thrilled. In case you are unhappy, do tell us. We will rebadge our employees handling your work on your payroll, so you can take over and run the show. Further, if you identify a different service provider, let us know to ensure a smooth transition without delay.' This frank conversation built trust in their minds, and they were willing to wait and watch—subject to the rider that there would be a review at frequent intervals.

The fourth and possibly the last reason was the board's swift measures to strengthen the management structure. For instance, we got Boston Consulting Group (BCG), a top management consulting firm, to support the board and advise the management. We promoted an insider, A.S. Murthy, as

CEO. We roped in Homi Khusrokhan and Partho Datta as special advisors. These were significant confidence-building measures for the customers.

BCG helped the board acquire an objective view of the business's cash-generating ability, accounting for the risks on the customer front. It advised the management to know the trend in declining revenues and cost reduction opportunities in operations. They were with us for four weeks. The two special advisors and BCG were passionate to be associated with the board in the larger cause of reviving Satyam and didn't want to be a cash burden on the company. They worked pro bono.

All this sent the right signal to the international market. Mark it—95 per cent of our customers operated from abroad!

◆

Customers were majorly bothered about the tainted image of Satyam. Americans are generally severe when it comes to their leaders and institutions breaching the confidence reposed in them. Former US President Bill Clinton's dalliance with Monica Lewinsky is a case in point. The complete annihilation of Arthur Andersen after the Enron scandal is another.

A few companies took an in-principle decision to part ways with us and asked their executives to find out how to terminate the contract without disrupting the project's continuity. Beyond a point, it was challenging to have any discussion with them.

Here, the fact that it is not easy for any customer to quit overnight in the IT industry became a big plus. We used this aspect to our advantage to reach out to the customers and persuade them to wait and watch for a few weeks.

We regularly got in touch with many customers by adopting some of these modes: (a) personal meeting at our headquarters, (b) deputing people to visit each jurisdiction to call on customers, and (c) seek conference call discussions. Satyam operated in 66 countries. So, we were connected to customers throughout the day and the night, depending on the time zone. In each meeting, we informed them of the steps taken on the matters in which they were most interested: restoration of financial stability, motivation measures to retain critical associates, steps executed to get a strategic investor to take over Satyam and the ability of the government-nominated board to ensure continuity of operations until it happened.

Most customers listened to us with respect and asked several questions. They were impressed by the speed with which India's government stepped into the scene and enabled six of us to take control with absolute independence and power. However, they wanted frequent updates. We agreed, lived up to our promise and passed on critical information in confidence that gave them immense faith in Satyam's revival.

Often, when negative news dripped in through the media, the customers panicked. They would call us ahead of the scheduled follow-up for an update. This was becoming quite a challenge. It was then that our marketing and communications team floated a weekly e-bulletin titled 'Source'. We circulated it among our clients worldwide, updating them on all the positive developments and explaining the negative fallout. We briefed them on the revival process and shared news of the fresh orders we had won. Clients liked the initiative and the regular flow of authentic information.

We told those willing to listen that our government was keen to protect customers and not allow any project to be derailed. Fortunately, no customer had any issue with the quality of service. Their worry was predominantly on the project's sustainability due to the financial crisis and the danger of disintegration of the execution team, who might jump ship. They were also mindful of the cost overrun if Satyam could not execute and the customer was forced to engage alternative service providers.

To get them on the same page as us, we had to ensure

undiminished qualitative delivery. This was a real challenge because of the demoralized workforce at various places. But with the motivation and confidence the board could give, the highly experienced and capable associates did it, and that is why in the end, Satyam was back on track.

◆

I toured the United Arab Emirates (UAE), covering Abu Dhabi, Dubai and Sharjah on 4 and 5 March 2009. Virender Aggarwal, regional business unit head for Asia Pacific and the Middle East, insisted that I, as a board member, visit the UAE.

I was in Hyderabad and had less than 24-hours' notice for the trip as the situation so demanded. My personal secretary, P. Balasundar, flew down from Chennai to Hyderabad with my passport, and I collected it at the airport before boarding the flight just in time!

So, on 4 March, along with Virender and other team members, I attended meetings organized with Dubai Silicon Oasis, Reuters Middle East, Abu Dhabi Aircraft Technologies, Sorouh Real Estate, Emirates Steel and Indian Farmers Fertiliser Cooperative Limited. The next day, we met the Al Rostamani Group, Emirates Trading Agency, Oracle, Emirates Bank, SAP and Dubai Insurance Group. They were very happy that one of the government-nominated board members along with the Satyam team personally called on them. There was positivity about continuing the relationship and patronizing the company in its most difficult period.

Satyam leaders Manish Mehta (head, SAP) and Sriram Papani (head, Enterprise Applications), flew down from India to join us in some of these meetings related to their verticals. Thus, over the two days, we could meet 10 groups of customers besides meeting SAP and Oracle, who were our vendors. Discussions with the Ajman government and Oman Insurance could not happen, which helped us spend extra time convincing other clients. On both days, unable to find time for lunch, we snacked while commuting.

During the meetings, the clients had several questions. We clarified operational issues. I did not have definite answers to their queries about the future, but I oozed confidence, and some of that passed on to them. Many customer organizations had Indian CAs in their finance and account teams. There were also Indian CFOs. Several of them recognized me either as their erstwhile teacher or as a former president of the ICAI, or both. This helped.

To motivate the team leadership and support staff and to send positive signals among the customer base, we organized a get-together in the evening on 4 March, followed by dinner at Seville's Restaurant, a Spanish outlet at Wafi City, Dubai. Many associates admitted they were smiling for the first time since 7 January. It was a refreshing and changed outlook for all the customers who turned up for the get-together. The entire tour, masterminded by Virender, was efficiently coordinated and accomplished.

That morning, Virender gave me 100 visiting cards with my designation as 'Satyam Director', saying, 'You will need them to exchange cards at the meetings.' When I left Dubai the next night, I noticed more than half of the cards exhausted. I was so happy when months later, I was told no customer from the jurisdiction turned their back on Satyam.

◆

There are two interesting stories I must tell you before we close out on how we retained customers. The first happened in February and the second in March.

On 23 February 2009, representatives of the NAB flew down to Hyderabad to hold discussions. I had mixed feelings about their trip. Would they call off the relationship? At the same time, I told myself, why would a high-profile team land up in person if they wanted to pull out? All of them were senior officers: Craig Bright, executive sponsor, Satyam Relationship; Dennis McGee, general manager, Business Technology Services; and Hamish McKenzie, head of Technology Partnering.

The Australians had come to understand the situation. NAB was positive and asked if they could lend a helping hand in addressing any risk. And they wanted to know our commitment to the Satyam–NAB relationship. I breathed easier. This was a morale booster, and we realized we were not alone in this battle. It gave us the confidence that many satisfied customers were willing to stand by Satyam. After the meeting ended, we had lunch along with a few members of the leadership team.

The second tale is of our multinational client, Nestlé. It deputed three of its topmost executives, viz., Belgian Paul Bulcke, CEO; Spaniard José Lopez, CFO; and Dutchman Frits van Dijk, zone head, to visit Bengaluru on 25 March to understand what was happening and decide the way forward. At that time, I was in Mumbai to negotiate terms with the bankers. I rushed to be in Garden City to join them for dinner at Leela Palace. Dr Keshab Panda from the leadership team was there from our side. We had a frank exchange of ideas for an hour. As we got down to wind up the conversation, the CEO told us his company would continue to patronize Satyam on the existing contract and allot new ones. The icing on the cake was when Paul said, 'If any client has questions about your company's ability to service, connect them to us; we can share our experience with them.'

That night, for the first time in many days, I had a sound and peaceful sleep. Four hours later, I took an early morning flight to Hyderabad to continue with the unfinished task.

◆

NEW WINS FROM EXISTING CUSTOMERS

Opportunity Won	Region	Industry	New/ Extension	TCV* ($Mn)	Duration (Years)
Customer 1	USA	Conglomerate	Extension & New	66	3
Customer 2	USA	Energy & Utilities	Extension	46	<1
Customer 3	USA	TIMES[1]	Extension	21	4
Customer 4	Rest of the World	Retail	New	18	7
Customer 5	Europe	Manufacturing	New	16	<1
Customer 6	Europe	Manufacturing	New	11	<1
Customer 7	Global	Manufacturing	Extension	9	<1
Customer 8	USA	ISV[2]	Extension	9	<1
Customer 9	Americas	Manufacturing	New	9	<1
Customer 10	USA	Energy & Utilities	Extension & New	6	<1
Others (205 Customers)				169	
*Total Contracted Value (from 215 customers)				$380 Mn	

Note: The names of customers have not been indicated as the information is confidential.

Between 7 January, when Satyam woke up to a crisis, and 31 March 2009, the company fought its way up. A third of existing customers (215 out of 654) helped by placing orders. From them, Satyam garnered a total contracted value of $380 million (₹18,240 crore). And 10 customers accounted for $211 million (₹10,128 crore)! From there, the recovery was bound to happen.

---

[1]Telecom, Infrastructure, Media and Entertainment, Semi-Conductor
[2]Independent software vendor

12

MANAGING MONEY WITHOUT DEFAULTS

On 18 January, the board received an SOS from the leadership team.

As described earlier, the team wanted confirmation that January salaries would be paid and sought an interim infusion of funds. It wanted a CEO to be appointed even if it were a temporary measure. These issues were addressed and fulfilled by the board.

However, the financial challenges continued beyond January and had to be managed holistically. The board had to meet fortnightly US salaries, month-end salaries in other geographies and outstanding statutory dues like taxes, PF dues, insurance, etc. As Satyam required ₹500 crore monthly towards payroll and ₹100 crore for administrative expenses, we were staring at the barrel of a gun, and the loans we received from the banks would only tide us over January.

Several payments were pending for materials supplied for the construction work-in-progress and capital expenditure in India, such as the supply of equipment, computers and furniture. So, matching cash inflows against outflows was a challenge. The daily cash statements had to be drawn, and payments were prioritized and released under my supervision. In all this, V. Ramesh Kumar, V.V.K. Raju and G. Subramanian, all senior finance men, complemented by V. Murali, did a splendid job. Special Advisor Partho Datta gave his expert guidance and wise counselling. We devised a five-pronged strategy and implemented it to secure the financial stability of Satyam. These were:

1. Gaining the confidence of the customers to receive overdue payments;
2. Deferment infrastructure projects capex;
3. Find ways to reduce or liquidate supplier dues;
4. Negotiate with bankers to restructure existing facilities;
5. Obtain a new bank loan to see Satyam does not suffer any unforeseen liquidity crunch.

Let's look at each one of them in turn.

GAINING THE CONFIDENCE OF CUSTOMERS

We won over customers little by little. Once customers showed their readiness to be with us, money started flowing in faster. Executives of each vertical also pushed for collections.

Some customers even paid the bills ahead of the usual credit period. For instance, if the amount was payable in 60 days, they settled it on the twentieth day itself. It's something we will never forget, and these gestures gave us a shot in the arm to pursue the task with renewed zeal. I realized that great customers bail out suppliers or service providers in times of distress and take the relationship to an entirely new level. Tarun helped reach out to the demanding customers through his network in foreign governments and friends among regulators. After that, outstanding bills started declining as payments began to flow in.

When we looked at the invoice to cash period, it was clear, Satyamites bounced back pretty fast. The pattern for January and February 2009 was not significantly different from April to December 2008. For the 11 months ending February 2009, 38 per cent of invoice value was collected within 30 days of billing, and another 35 per cent within 45 days. Debtors exceeding 90 days were a tiny 7 per cent. Consequently, for the first two months, namely January and February, the company paid salaries and statutory dues only from internal accruals. However, loan amounts drawn from IDBI Bank and BoB gave us the comfort of meeting the obligations without any anxiety or uncertainty. At that point, I silently thanked the customers for patronizing Satyam in turbulent times, facilitating payment of salaries and statutory liabilities only out of internal accruals.

DEFERMENT OF INFRASTRUCTURE PROJECTS CAPEX

At the board meeting held on 21 February, we considered one agenda extensively. That was relating to 'infrastructure facilities under construction'. The company secretary presented the status report about the ongoing projects of the company. The board noted that four projects were under development, and only Phase I of these projects was being implemented. The cost incurred so far was ₹322.47 crore, of which ₹74.75 crore was due to the vendors.

Among these four projects, the board noted that SLC3 at STC, Hyderabad, required only ₹1.5 crore to complete Phase I for accommodating 678 workstations. We, therefore, cleared its completion. The other projects were deferred, and the board decided to settle the dues of ₹74.75 crore through negotiations and bargaining.

SQUARING UP LIABILITIES

In material suppliers and equipment suppliers, we identified the payments due to assets already put to use. We quickly settled them.

Where the materials were not required immediately, we requested the supplier to take them back. We obtained the SEZ authorities' approval to return capital goods without duty payment. I wrote to the development commissioner of SEZ seeking authorization to do so. In that letter I reasoned that:

> Due to global recession, there is a change in the project schedule after receiving some imported and indigenous capital goods against orders released based on initial project plans. Satyam has not used many items so far and is also yet to pay the suppliers. To avoid technological obsolescence and protect the warranty of the equipment, the suppliers were willing to take back the material from Satyam, thereby reducing immediate liability and agreed to supply the material with the latest technology as and when required.

This proposal was approved, and we could return all those materials and equipment without any duty obligations.

V. Murali (head, Commercial) led a task force on settling dues to vendors, service providers and suppliers. The team carried out long-drawn negotiations, squeezing out substantial discounts and some easy monthly options. Somewhere along the line, Murali dinned into the suppliers to accept what was being offered. Soon, they realized something is better than nothing and ungrudgingly picked what was offered.

This was when I realized every rupee saved is a rupee earned.

NEGOTIATE WITH BANKS FOR RESTRUCTURING EXISTING FACILITIES

Our bankers were exerting pressure for recovering the amounts due. We held several rounds of talks with their team to prevent recovery proceedings from being initiated. One of the banks unilaterally transferred our money lying in its account in different countries, including Singapore, into the account in India and adjusted it against our dues. This jeopardized our liquidity and it had the Satyam head in Singapore running for cover. When he realized the bank balance in Singapore was wiped out, he made a frantic call to us on a Friday, saying that unless welfare dues, insurance and taxes were remitted on Monday, he could get arrested as per local laws. We acted fast to ensure the restoration of money to the bank account and thus prevent such undesirable consequences.

We had several sittings with Citibank and BNP in Hyderabad and Mumbai to convince them to continue to support us with revised terms. It consumed a lot of time to reach an understanding and execute the modified agreements. The loan arrangements with HDFC Bank and HSBC were renegotiated cordially. The completion of this exercise, despite the ordeal we went through, gave us breathing space.

OBTAIN FRESH LOANS FROM BANKS

The board decided to look for a working capital loan as a stopgap arrangement to meet any unforeseen contingency. IDBI and BoB came forward to sanction ₹300 crore each, in February, thanks to Deepak's efforts. The kind of goodwill and reputation Deepak enjoyed in the corporate world in general and the banking industry, in particular, was incredible. The teams of both banks arrived at the campus, and the process of collating necessary documents began.

I worked on operational details with commercial head V. Murali and with the finance trio of V.V.K. Raju, Ramesh Kumar and G. Subbu. I kept Deepak posted, and he chipped in with pieces of sage advice. Partho pitched in with his wise counsel. These included documentation for a mortgage of the two campuses, the valuation of the fixed assets by authorized valuation experts and getting a no objection certificate from APIIC for mortgaging the Hi-Tech City property of Satyam.

On 2 February, the Income Tax Department provisionally attached the properties. This was due to a reopening of assessments for earlier years and the likely demands that might arise. So, we now also had to get a no objection certificate from the Income Tax Department! I wrote to Ajay Mishra, IAS, requesting concurrence through APIIC to allow Satyam to raise short-term loans on the security of Satyam's land in Hi-Tech City. A copy was marked to the managing director of APIIC, Government of Andhra Pradesh. After a meticulous follow-up, the concurrence letter arrived. I submitted a review petition and letters to the commissioner of income tax to issue a no objection certificate. I met the authorities, and they suggested I represent before the director general of income tax (Investigation) Amalendu Das. I did so on 25 February. The next day, the tax department permitted to create a charge on Satyam's properties in favour of IDBI and BoB.

We also had a technical search carried out in the sub-registrar's office, so the bank officers could verify if we held a perfect title to them. Finally, we went to Mumbai and negotiated and finalized various loan documents to be executed with the banks. The legal teams prepared and vetted the documents, after which the agreement was inked. By the time all this could be done, it was the end of February 2009. Until then, we managed to pay salaries and statutory dues out of collections from customers.

In February, we drew 50 per cent of loans sanctioned. Consequently, we paid interest only on ₹300 crore; ₹150 crore each from IDBI and BoB, leaving the balance ₹300 crore undrawn. Similarly, HDFC sanctioned a new loan of ₹85 crore, of which we drew ₹69 crore. We knew we should not spend it in a hurry just because we had access to money. After all, it was the bank's money!

The loans from IDBI and BoB gave us immense strength in working towards Satyam's revival. For the first time, we felt confident we would not default on any payment. My respect for public-sector banks went sky-high because they came forward to support this mission. On 4 April, Partho and I were at his Ballard Pier office to thank M.D. Mallya, chairman and managing director of BoB. Later, in 2018, Mallya passed away. We also met and thanked Jitender Balakrishnan, deputy managing director, and S. Ananthakrishnan, executive director of IDBI Bank, at their Cuffe Parade office. Little did I know then that the government would invite me to head one such bank six years later! In 2015, I took charge as chairman, Canara Bank. Interestingly, on 9 May 2022, I took charge as chairman, IDBI Bank with the approval of the RBI.

During March 2009, all current obligations were cleared, and long-pending dues were either amicably settled or paid out. It wiped out the tarnished image of Satyam. It improved the confidence level of associates, customers, vendors, service providers and suppliers in Satyam. Above all, it convinced the prospective strategic investors keenly evaluating the option of acquiring Satyam that we were alive and kicking.

CASH FLOWS (9 JANUARY–31 MARCH 2009)

We collected reasonable amounts of money from customers, and paid salaries and statutory liabilities on time. We also renegotiated terms with bankers, vendors, and others, raised new loans, took appropriate calls on forex exposure management and drove cost optimization. The resultant cash flow is given below.

Rs Crore

Cash Flow Summary	January[1]	February	March	Grand Total
Opening Balance A	143	300	482	143
Collections B	736	636	692	2,064
Loans C	–	300	69	369
Payments D	579	754	870	2,203
Surplus/deficit (B+C-D) E	157	182	(109)[2]	230
Closing balance (A+E)	300	482	373	373

---

[1]From 9th till 31st January

[2]It is a negative number, implying that the inflow during the month is less than the payments in that month. (B+C-D) is negative.

PART 6

SELECTING THE INVESTOR

13

PRE-BID APPROVALS AND MEDIATION

Within 50 days of Raju's explosive letter, we knew the worst was over.

By the end of February 2009, we had both employees and customers on our side. Our associates stopped wearing a hangdog expression and were sufficiently pumped up and itching to take Satyam back to its former glory. Most of our customers had shown faith in us by staying with us during these troubled times. Once they realized Raju had perpetrated an accounting fraud on shareholders and not an operations scam on either employees or customers, the mood changed. They were also taken by the government's serious intent and the intensity with which the new board worked.

To use a medical analogy, Satyam could be relieved of the ventilator support but had to stay in the intensive care unit (ICU). Yes, it could breathe easier but was not yet fit to move to the regular ward.

The only thing left for Satyam was to find a white knight. In business, a white knight is a friendly investor who acquires a company with support from the board. We had some probing questions. Which knight in shining armour would come to save the damsel in distress? Which knight would infuse capital and helm the management of the company? We had to scout and find out.

◆

Earlier, the internationally well-known Goldman Sachs, and the domestic rising star Avendus, had been appointed as investment bankers to help on all transactions leading up to the bidding.

We started to focus on getting approvals and exemptions for initiating bidding. The legal advisors and the investment bankers worked on it under the guidance of Achuthan, who was a treasure trove of knowledge and experience.

On 23 January, we applied to SEBI seeking certain relaxations under Regulation 20(4) of the SEBI Takeover Regulations for initiating the process of identifying a strategic investor. We requested SEBI to exempt Satyam from the SEBI formula that would determine the floor price for takeover. This was because the formula is based on market price, and given the flawed balance sheet of Satyam, the market price was unreliable. We also wanted an exemption from putting up the latest financial data as these were unaudited, and, more importantly, questionable.

On 13 February, SEBI notified an amendment to the SEBI Takeover Regulations, introducing Regulation 29A, which took care of what we wanted.

Five days later, on 18 February, we applied before the CLB, seeking several reliefs, including permission to increase Satyam's authorized capital and make a preferential allotment of shares without convening an annual general meeting of the company. As any strategic investor wants adequate equity shareholding to constitute its board, a preferential allotment must be made. Such an allotment would cross the existing authorized capital of Satyam, and hence the company must increase it.

The very next day, the CLB accepted our request. Its order dated 19 February 2009 laid out reasons for relaxations and the necessary conditions to be followed. Among other things, it stated that Satyam required funds and managerial expertise to do well in the long term. The CLB authorized Satyam to amend the capital clause to increase the authorized share capital from ₹160 crore comprising equity shares of ₹2 each to ₹280 crore.

The resolution so passed would be deemed done in a general meeting under Section 17 of the Companies Act, 1956. The CLB also authorized Satyam to make a preferential allotment of equity shares and allowed the resolution to be deemed a special resolution passed in a general meeting under Section 81(1A) of the Act. Under the law then prevailing, contained in Section 81, any new shares must first be offered to existing shareholders. This offer is referred to as a Rights Offer. However, by passing a special resolution of the company in a general meeting, the shareholders can forego this right and invite others to subscribe to the additional capital.

The CLB order meant that we did not have to go to the shareholders for approval.

Most importantly, the order allowed us to induct a strategic investor through a competitive process overseen by a retired judge of the Supreme Court or a former Chief Justice of India. Legal eagle K. Parasaran, the Solicitor General, appearing for the Union of India, supported our application.

To comply with the CLB directive, we shortlisted four men whose words we thought would count. One of them did not respond and another declined. Fortunately, Justice Sam Piroj Bharucha accepted our invitation, so there was no need to reach out to the fourth. An advocate, a former Chief Justice of the Karnataka High Court, and later the Chief Justice of India, Justice Bharucha, 72, was widely respected.

On 27 February, a consolidated application under Regulation 29A of the SEBI Takeover Regulations was made for permission to grant relaxations of specific provisions of Chapter III of the SEBI Takeover Regulations. The relaxations included:

1. Dispensation from publishing disclosures;
2. Statutory auditor's certificate for certifying compliance with SEBI (Disclosure and Investor Protection) Guidelines;

3. Time limits for allotment of shares on a preferential basis;
4. Eligibility criteria of the allottee; and
5. Exemption from the application of minimum open offer price for the public offer.

The relaxations were sought since Satyam did not have audited financial statements. Mark it; the earlier auditors, PW, had signed, later issued a disclaimer of opinion and subsequently resigned. We left the appointment of the new auditor to the incoming strategic investor. Satyam was a crisis situation, making normal norms and timelines in takeover regulations difficult to adopt. Therefore, we requested for the above-mentioned relaxations.

We sought permission to proceed with the price bid auction without floor price, with an absolute right reserved to the Satyam board to reject all the bids that were not acceptable.

On 3 March, SEBI gave an in-principle approval subject to specific observations. It relaxed takeover norms for this case, rapidly drafting and pushing through necessary amendments.

Our board met every week and closely monitored the progress. As the regulators, the investment bankers and Justice Bharucha were based in Mumbai, we met in India's financial capital on bidding matters. Deepak allowed us to use the premises of HDFC on three occasions, viz., 12 February, 21 March and 9 April.

Let me share a personal experience of working with Deepak. Quick in grasping, sharp in analysing and expeditious in decision-making, he was the person many looked up to for guidance, inspiration and emulation. During the board meetings at Hyderabad, most of our stay was at ITC Grand Kakatiya. There, I found that while Satyam had booked a standard room for Deepak and us, the hotel had voluntarily upgraded him to a presidential suite. It was an indication of the stature and standing he enjoyed in the public eye. I would bask in reflected glory, thrilled at working with him. I would wonder if I, too, could achieve this. Years later, let me share with humility, it happened to me several times at the same hotel. It's good to be in the company of high achievers—the law of attraction works.

In the meantime, an advocate, Manohar Lal Sharma, moved a writ petition before the Delhi High Court challenging the issuing of preferential allotment of shares to the strategic investor without offering the same to the existing shareholders. We felt relieved when the petition was dismissed in March 2009.[1]

As the process of inviting strategic investors was going on, the board decided to discontinue BCG's services. BCG had done a remarkable job, and the fact that they did it without a fee did not in any way reduce their enthusiasm for the assignment. At the meeting held on 5 March, the board recorded its appreciation of the consulting major's excellent work.

The investment bankers made a presentation on the bidding transaction process, indicating the stages crossed and still pending. We reviewed the proposed timelines and felt reassured that things were moving on expected lines.

◆

Meanwhile, there was Upaid, a UK-based company, whose claims had to be settled. In April 2007, in the US, Upaid had taken Satyam to court alleging fraud, forgery and breach of contract involving the transfer of intellectual property (IP) rights. The dispute was related to a project the two worked on together in the late 1990s. The UK company had sought damages of a billion dollars.

We agreed to meet representatives of Upaid and, like gentlemen, discuss it across the table.

---

[1] 'CLB Nod to Satyam for Inducting Investor Challenged in SC', *The Economic Times*, 24 February 2009, https://bit.ly/3S00IfY. Accessed on 26 July 2022; 'SC Dismisses Plea Against Satyam', *Financial Express*, 5 January 2010, https://bit.ly/3PNzEPi. Accessed on 26 July 2022.

Rajat Gupta, the former managing director of McKinsey & Company, and Raj Mitta, a board member of the Guardian group, represented Upaid in mediation. Simon Joyce, chairman and CEO of Upaid, joined them. Legal Advisor Pallavi Shroff, Commercial Head V. Murali, Santosh Nair from Satyam Legal and I represented Satyam. The meeting was held over two days on 9 and 10 March at Four Seasons Hotel, Mumbai.

After a deadlock on the first day, I updated Tarun, Kiran and Deepak about the negotiations. While Tarun gave a few strategic inputs to square up the liability and Kiran wished me well, Deepak cautioned we should not burden the new investor with a huge settlement. I assured Deepak it wouldn't happen. Deepak asked me to go ahead but hinted that beyond a point, I should quietly withdraw. After all, other vital items awaited my attention, such as concluding the arrangements with bankers and compiling information sought by investment bankers to be furnished to the bidders at appropriate stages.

After several rounds of conversation, Upaid was willing to pare down its demand of $100 million by 10 per cent, namely by $10 million. However, we conceded to pay a maximum of $10 million. A 10 per cent discount versus a 90 per cent concession! So, there could hardly be any meeting halfway.

We mediated because if settled for a reasonable amount, it would maximize the value for Satyam shareholders. After all, any potential investor would pay higher if the Damoclean sword of a billion-dollar suit didn't hang above Satyam. At the same time, we didn't want to fasten a considerable liability on the buyer. Since there was no significant development, there was no point in carrying on with the negotiation.

Rajat, Raj and I shook hands and walked away as friends, leaving it to the new investor to take the call. We had wanted to square up one law suit to maximize the value, but that was not to be. We left it to the new investors to negotiate and settle, which is how it happened later.

TRANSACTION PROCESS AND TIMELINE (PROPOSED PLAN)

	Process Steps	Key Activities	Timeline (Days)
1	Apply to SEBI for process approval	Submit application to SEBI and intimate CLB	T[2]
2	Receive SEBI approval	SEBI to issue a notification	T + 2
3	Publish request for Expression of Interest (EOI)	• RFP[3] to be published on the website of Satyam, BSE, NSE, Goldman Sachs and Avendus Capital • Articulate pre-qualification criteria • RFP to contain the standard draft Share Subscription Agreement (SSA)	T + 2
4	Receive EOIs from potential bidders	• Collect relevant supporting documents from bidders (proof of financial capacity, strategic plan for Satyam, etc.) • Receive comments on SSA, if any, and circulate non-negotiable draft	T + 9
5	Evaluate EOIs on the basis of pre-qualification criteria	Shortlist bidders	T + 19
6	Inform shortlisted bidders and complete pre due-diligence formalities	Bidders to sign Auction Participation Agreement, Non-Disclosure Agreement, Standstill Agreement, and Process Confidentiality Agreement (Right to disqualify bidder midway the process for any breach of confidentiality)	T + 20
7	Commence due-diligence	• Share information pack • Conduct monitored management presentation • Identify shortlisted bidders who wish to make a bid	T + 21

---

[2]T stands for today. So, T+2 means two days from today, etc. Here, it will mean that if we place the application on, say, 19 August, the next one, T+2, is on 21 August.
[3]Request for proposal

	Process Steps	Key Activities	Timeline (Days)
8	Receive sealed bids	Bidders to send in binding sealed bids post due diligence along with a ₹100 crore commitment fee (to be forfeited if winning bidder does not honour bid)	T + 31
9	Commence auction process	Based on number of bids received, decide on the format of auction process	T + 33
10	Select successful bidder	The board, after confirmation with retired Supreme Court Justice, announces the successful bidder	T + 33
11	Successful bidder to deposit 100 per cent cash for subscribing to the preferential allotment	Money comes in the designated account of Satyam	T + 37
12	Execute SSA	Company executes the SSA with the successful bidder	T + 37

14

SWAYAMVARAM

On 9 March, Satyam kick-started the registration process. Formally, the race to bring in the suitor had begun.

We invited corporates to register if they wished to bid for Satyam. The cut-off date for registration, indicating that they were interested in participating in the process of selection, was 5 p.m. on 12 March. We received 141 registrations. Some of them were fictitious, and some applied for the heck of it. The irony was that a few miscreants even registered in the name of Rajus, as though his family was eyeing to acquire Satyam!

By 13 March, we got back to all those whose email IDs and registration details could be verified and gave them a request for proposal (RFP) document. The RFP outlined how registered bidders could submit their Expression of Interest (EOI). Among other things, we wanted the bidders to file their audited financial statements for the past three years. We also wanted proof that they had ₹1,500 crore to back their bid. While they could borrow money to fund the acquisition, they would have to share both the source and time frame. The RFP provided disqualification criteria and the process of selecting the successful bidder. Reasons for disqualification included the inability to provide proof of the availability of ₹1,500 crore (approximately $290 million) or evidence of the ability to pay the total acquisition funds within four days after being declared the winner.

It laid out that each qualified bidder would have to submit two sealed envelopes upon completion of the due diligence process. The first would contain relevant information relating to technical criteria. The second would contain a financial bid setting forth the subscription price per share, along with details of the sources of financing.

As a result of SEBI's relaxations, there would be no floor price for the financial bids.

In consultation with Justice Bharucha, the board would shortlist qualified bidders based on the technical criteria. Such criteria included experience in IT and IT-related services, size and scale of operations, credentials in governance, and a track record of running a global-level business. Evidence of experience in turnaround, corporate social responsibility (CSR) spending and the quality of a proposed strategic plan for Satyam were given weightage.

After that, the board and Justice Bharucha would open the shortlisted bidders' financial bids to determine the winner. If the second-highest bid was less than 90 per cent of the highest bid, the highest bidder would be declared a successful bidder. Otherwise, there would be an additional round of sealed bids among those bidders. After that, the board, in consultation with Justice Bharucha, would declare the bidder who submitted the highest bid in the second round as the successful bidder.

A condition was stipulated that the buyer should not sell Satyam assets or Satyam as an entity for two years from the date of completion of the public offer unless consent by special resolution was obtained. The idea was to prevent anyone from acquiring Satyam with an eye at asset stripping and not sustaining the business. There was also a three-year lock-in period of the shares allotted in pursuance of the bid to discourage bargain hunters.

The deadline for submission of EOI was 20 March at 5 p.m. At the closing bell, 10 documents were received. Justice Bharucha and the board evaluated them the following day and found three of them incomplete.

The seven qualified bidders were now given a few pre-transaction documents, such as the Non-Disclosure Agreement, Standstill Agreement and Process Confidentiality Agreement. Those who executed these agreements and provided an irrevocable performance bank guarantee of ₹5 crore would get access to due diligence information, including a virtual data room containing the company's story. They would also attend a presentation by the senior management of Satyam in Hyderabad.

Out of the seven eligible bidders, documents from two were not received, as it appears they could not get approvals from their shareholders. Thus, only five bidders stayed in the race, viz., L&T, Tech Mahindra, Cognizant, WL Ross & Co. and Spice Group.

On 23 March, these companies were issued a bid process letter, containing process details and technical criteria for submitting the technical bid.

Under requirements of the US Securities Act 1934, a detailed note setting out the competitive bidding process, a statement of relaxations applied for from SEBI under Regulation 29A and the text of the in-principle approval granted by SEBI was filed with the SEC. It was also filed with SEBI on 24 March. We confirmed that the entire process was formulated in consultation with SEBI.

As the due diligence process began, we started to provide the shortlisted bidders access to financial, legal and client information. We told them to make an independent assessment of the pending class-action lawsuits in the US. They were welcome to speak to our legal counsel but were told that neither Satyam nor its counsel would be able to provide an estimate of the potential claim in class-action suits.

Even as the buyers were busy doing due diligence on us, we wanted to do due diligence on their reputational background. And through the investment bankers, we engaged Kroll, a New York-based corporate investigations and risk consulting firm, which would carry out reputational due diligence of the bidders.

The Spice Group, one of the five shortlisted, had several problems with the bidding. Among others, they wanted open bidding.

Let me digress a bit here to explain both open and closed bidding.

In open bidding, every bidder knows who the competitor is and how much they are bidding. This allows them to make counter bids. It would be like an Indian Premier League (IPL) or a Sotheby auction, where multiple offers by the same person are possible. The open bid process is fair if bidders have asymmetrical information about a product or a company. In that case, the least-informed bidder could at least decide his bid price based on what others quote. But at Satyam, everyone was equally well-informed or ill-informed, including the management! There was no point in making an open bid.

In closed bidding, a participant makes a one-time offer in a sealed bid and doesn't know what others have quoted. The auctioneer reveals the price at the end of the auction. The one who placed the highest bid wins. When bidders cannot see offers made by competitors, all bidders have a fair chance to win a bid based on predetermined criteria.

Let me get back to our story.

Many board members received calls from a director in the Spice Group seeking information on other bidders. When we refused to divulge anything, citing these were confidential, the group began publicly discrediting the bidding procedure. We didn't blink. By the way, none of the other bidders had issues with these matters. Spice took the case to Justice Bharucha, who ruled in the board's favour. Finally, Spice decided to stay away from the bidding process.[1]

---

[1] These calls were recorded by directors, which also included T.N. Manoharan.

Cognizant Technologies, who submitted an EOI, subsequently informed the board that they would be acting as a 'person in concert' with WL Ross & Co. In law, a person in concert means someone who collaborates with another for acquiring shares or voting rights in a company to obtain effective control of that company.

In the end, only three bidders, viz., L&T, Tech Mahindra and WL Ross & Co. remained in the race. On 24 March, we created a virtual data room. There, we put out information on the third quarter's financials ending December 2008, the profit and loss statement of January and February 2009, and the top line of March 2009. A summary of the top 100 contracts was also provided. We laid bare details of the tangible and intangible assets, the liabilities and obligations, HR-related information, legal cases pending and related claims. The eligible bidders were given access to the virtual data room subject to their furnishing guarantees on confidentiality, etc., from 25 March onwards.

On 27, 28 and 29 March, Satyam's senior management team conducted presentations to the prospective bidders. We also facilitated campus visits.

During the presentations, the bidders asked several questions. Tech Mahindra was led by veteran Vineet Nayyar, managing director and CEO. L&T had Y.M. Deosthalee, CFO and board member, shepherding his team. WL Ross was represented by Ranjeet Nabha and an associate.

The management gave clarifications immediately, and in some cases, sought time. The management videographed both the presentation and the interaction to ensure there were no discriminations in sharing inputs between various bidders. Whatever information was provided based on a query from one bidder was passed on to the other two bidders.

As the new financial year began, I began to see a ray of hope—the bidding process was heading in the right direction. On 2 April, based on discussions with advisors and

Justice Bharucha, the board amended the process of financial bids. If any of the offers were within 90 per cent of the highest bid, we laid out that a follow-up open auction, and not sealed-cover bidding, would be conducted among those bidders. It meant that if the best bid was ₹40, and the second best was ₹36, then open bidding—IPL style—would follow between those two bidders. This would be carried out after a two-hour break so that the bidders could talk to their decision-makers to deploy a strategy. All bidders, SEBI and stock exchanges were duly informed of these changes. Everyone agreed.

The bidders wanted to have a sitting with the board to get clarity on certain ambiguities and to obtain further information. We scheduled a meeting on 3 April at The Taj Mahal Palace Hotel, Colaba. Separate slots were given to the three bidders to appear independently, and we responded to all their doubts.

Whatever additional input they requested was prepared on a war footing on 4 and 5 April and hosted in the virtual data room. While they did not want an extension of time to submit the bids, the trio hinted that a few more days would help. So, we shifted the bid date from 9 April to 13 April.

Earlier, we fixed different slots for teleconference calls, with a separate call for finance-related matters and another for legal issues. So, with three bidders in the fray, we had six calls! A lot of effort went into culling the data relating to various aspects of the company to meet their queries. These calls happened on 2, 4 and 7 April with the bidders' legal counsels and financial advisors.

At the board meeting of 9 April, I felt the intense pressure of facing an upcoming examination. With 96 hours to go for the big day, I had butterflies in my stomach. The board members discussed with the investment bankers and legal advisors key aspects for conducting the 13 April auction. The board was satisfied that the process was open, fair and competitive. Justice Bharucha gave us the thumbs up.

During this period, the legal advisors shared draft versions of transaction documents with the bidders. These documents were finalized on 10 April. The bidders submitted signed copies of these agreements between 10 and 11 April. Further, till 12 April, the virtual data room continued to host updated information on the company's operations.

We didn't formally discuss it, but I expected a price in the range of ₹50–70 per share.

Let's now step into the last over of Satyam's revival.

MANAGEMENT PRESENTATION TO BIDDERS ON 27, 28 AND 29 MARCH 2009

Opening remarks by Homi Khusrokhan and Partho Datta in turns

'Pleasant good morning, everyone.

What CEO A.S. Murthy and his team will try to do over the next three hours is to take you through a whistle-stop tour of what a group of people, which is still amazingly intact and who are today led by him, have done. From a zero base in just over two decades by (a) sheer hard work and commitment, (b) the teamwork of an extraordinary order, and (c) a unique culture of entrepreneurial leadership, they have created a set of differentiated offerings and a set of skills and expertise that is even today considered to be among the best in class, globally.

The purpose of the presentation is to give you a feel of the value that this team has built, a value firmly embedded in Satyam, a value that will sustain and a value that can further be built.

Admittedly, the Company today is in 'music-minus-one' mode, but again, through a relatively unique combination of interim leadership of a high order; expert guidance; and support from the highest levels of government and regulators like SEBI, it has been fortunate to have been put on the revival path very rapidly by restoring financial and operational stability leading to preservation of values and wealth.

As a person who has now spent a considerable amount of time working with this team, I can say that there is a strong belief that this Company can be rebuilt and can regain its past glory. The group appears to be on the job 24/7, and I sometimes wonder if they sleep at all.

Through my four-five interactions with the customers of this Company, I have found that there is still a tremendous amount of confidence customers continue to repose in them, which is one of their greatest strengths. This will come through strongly in the presentation. The customer bonds that this Company has created and the high degree of operational excellence they have developed would take a new entrant many years, if not decades, to recreate.

Finally, I have found through my interaction, particularly with people from India's corporate world, that many are waiting and watching how the story unfolds. Today is beginning to see the makings of a success story. I also sense that there is a lot of goodwill and sympathy out there for the people of Satyam. This goodwill amazingly extends beyond India's shores, and there is a tremendous following Satyam enjoys in countries like Malaysia, Egypt and Australia.

Many recognize Satyam has been associated with good things in the past, and ultimately the good must be preserved. At the same time, the bad must be expunged from the organization.

Therefore, the good wishes of many well-wishers are assured at this challenging time, which is a very satisfying feeling. We need the good wishes and blessings of all. And of course, some luck, so that we succeed in finding a perfect fit with the right strategic investor!

I will now hand over to ASM and his team to make a presentation. I will, from time to time, intersperse with my outside-in remarks and observations, when necessary.'

Presentation by CEO A.S. Murthy and his team

CEO Murthy made presentations on the revival. Rajan Nagarajan spoke on governance and financial management, T.R. Anand on customers and A.S. Murthy on employees. Homi and Partho steered the question-and-answer [Q&A] session that followed these presentations.

After a tea break, it was back to the presentation. Dr Keshab Panda and Manish Mehta outlined Satyam's strong fundamentals and business strengths. Murali presented financial information comprising revenues from January to March, 2009, liabilities and cash flows. Murthy, Homi and Partho spoke passionately on Satyam's CSR activities covering Satyam Foundation, EMRI and HMRI. Murthy also explained about arrangement with FIFA-World Cup Football event for which Satyam provides the technical support.

Concluding Observations

Towards the end, both Homi and Partho highlighted where the strategic investor can bring in value.

'Put in place a new road map, restore Satyam to its high-growth chart and establish highest levels of corporate governance. Leverage Satyam's pull on customers, bring in a strong bottom-line focus, and, above all, preserve the Company's spirit of engagement in CSR.'

The duo, given their vast corporate experience, sounded out on optimizing bench strength, monetization of land bank and revival of Satyam BPO. They also suggested a relook at the JVs [joint ventures] for synergy and closure, redesigning the organization structure and rationalizing office space. In their view, one word sums up what is needed, viz. 'coruscation'. In the jewellery industry, the word means restoring the glitter and sparkle of an old gem.

However, the most poignant words came in the end, and rightfully so.

'Some of Satyam's most loyal customers have even come forward to say that they would be prepared to speak with other customers on behalf of the management and tell them how satisfied they have been with Satyam.' And added, 'What this company needs is an investor who believes in their strengths and will work with them to restore Satyam back to its early glory.'

15
THE WINNER

13 April 2009

Venue: Taj President, Mumbai

Attendees

Board members: Kiran Karnik, Deepak Parekh, Tarun Das, C. Achuthan, S. Balakrishna Mainak and T.N. Manoharan

Special invitees: Justice Bharucha, Homi Khusrokhan and Partho Datta

Goldman Sachs: Richard Breeden, Brooks Entwistle, Sunil Sanghai, Sudarshan Ramakrishnan, Riddhesh Gandhi and Ankur Trehen

Avendus Capital Services: Ranu Vohra, Kaushal Aggarwal, Amit Singh, Aditya Khurana and Gaurav Singhal

Amarchand & Mangaldas & Suresh A. Shroff & Co: Shardul Shroff, Pallavi Shroff, Dharini Mathur, Natashaa Shroff, Amit Agarwal and Rahul Singh

Bidders: J.P. Nayak, Venkatesan Narasimhan and N. Sivaraman (L&T); Jatin Berry and Manoj Bhat (Tech Mahindra); Ranjeet Nabha, Surya Mahadev and Apurva Diwanji (WL Ross)

◆

For my colleagues and me on the Satyam board, this was the D-Day. We would not just get to know who gets to own Satyam but also whether our work over the past 97 days would meet corporate approbation. As we sat in the ballroom in Taj President, my mind raced back in time.

I remembered Anurag Goel calling me on the handset to check my availability to sit on Satyam's board. I recalled being in awe of the infrastructure at Satyam when I first visited its corporate office. I played back the various pep talks board members gave to heartbroken employees. The customer calls we held, through the day and night on many days, lingered in my mind. I couldn't forget my visits to the Middle East to rebuild friendships with our clients. I got reminded of the long discussions with our hard-nosed bankers to have a few conditions changed. All of this was hopefully coming to a happy closure. And how could I forget the meet with the associates?

I had this practice of meeting the associates of each vertical every week to interact with them. In the week preceding the bid, at a meet with the team that works on Oracle, I said Satyam would have a new owner on 13 April. In the Q&A session, one of the associates raised his hand and said, 'One last question, please.'

We were past the agreed time, but I allowed him. 'Manoharan, what would happen if nobody turns up for the bid?'

At that moment, my heart skipped a beat. The thought had never crossed my mind. Perhaps it had to do with our board's confidence. For us, the board, it was unthinkable, after doing all we did to restore financial stability, customer retention and employee motivation, that no one would pick the country's fourth-largest technology company. But yes, this was a valid question. True, we had slogged the last 97 days, given our tears, sweat and toil. But what would happen if no one came to the party?

I thought for a few seconds, the longest few seconds of my life, and then I smiled, 'If no one turns up, we will execute Plan B.' I had pulled this out of thin air, but it instilled confidence in the hall. The group cheered and dispersed. The associate didn't ask, 'What's your Plan B?' If he had, I would have said, 'Wait and watch!'

These memories danced before me that morning as I waited in the Taj President, for the bid to begin.

◆

One by one, the dramatis personae checked in.

C. Achuthan, our go-to director on matters relating to SEBI and Company Law, lived in Mumbai and arrived at 8.45 a.m.

Next to drop in was S. Balakrishna Mainak, the LIC's nominee on the Satyam board. He, too, lived in Mumbai, attended all our board meetings and kept himself available for a couple of days a week in Hyderabad whenever I travelled out on work. Kiran Karnik, our chairman, and the incredibly networked Tarun Das, who lived in New Delhi, had checked into the hotel the previous day. I had taken the evening flight from Chennai and checked into Room 1507.

Deepak Parekh, the 'Badshah of Banking', drove into Taj President at 9 a.m. along with the man of the moment, Justice Bharucha.

Seeing these men, a few more thoughts of the last 12 weeks passed through my mind. I recalled how our board meetings were always held unconventionally: brainstorming, discussing and debating to reach a conclusion, with advisors chipping in. There was never a case of one-upmanship, and we always had unanimity in decision-making.

13 April was to be our pay day.

Seeing the representatives of L&T, Tech Mahindra and WL Ross, I breathed a sigh of relief. Thank God the bidders had come! The nightmare of a 'no-show' had been averted.

Cognizant, who were to participate through WL Ross & Co., as person acting in concert, had opted out at the eleventh hour.

Even as I sat thinking, the bidders were invited, in turn, to submit their proposals.

My next worry was whether we would get a reasonable price. The previous day, a professor teaching corporate valuation to a group of executives said the best price to offer would be the average market price since 7 January, plus a premium to get controlling interest. When quizzed what should be the premium, he indicated, 'Anywhere between 25 per cent and 33 per cent.' That would be between ₹54 and ₹58.

Infrastructure major L&T held a 12 per cent stake in Satyam. Earlier, in December 2008, it had a 3.95 per cent stake. After Raju's confession, it gradually acquired more shares to reach its present level.

L&T Chairman Anil Naik wanted Satyam in their portfolio, come hell or high water. The company submitted its bid at 9.15 a.m. Chairman Karnik, Justice Bharucha and L&T representatives signed the envelopes on the reverse. After signing, L&T handed over the bids to Karnik.

Part of the Mahindra group, Tech Mahindra, was a niche player working on software telecom. In contrast, Satyam was in a wide range of software verticals. An acquisition would make a lot of sense to them. Tech Mahindra participated in the bid process through its wholly owned subsidiary Venturbay Consultants Private Limited and submitted its bid at 9.25 a.m. through its representatives. Chairman Karnik, Justice Bharucha, and Tech Mahindra representatives signed the envelopes on the reverse. After the signing, Tech Mahindra formally presented the bids to Chairman Karnik.

WL Ross & Co. (India Asset Recovery Fund), the domestic arm of the well-known US-based private equity fund, buys financially distressed companies and turns them around. WL Ross submitted its bid at 9.55 a.m. Chairman Karnik,

Justice Bharucha and WL Ross representatives signed the bid envelopes on the reverse. After signing, WL Ross formally presented them to Chairman Karnik.

Each bid had to be evaluated for its technical competence. Between 10.15 a.m. and 11.00 a.m., the board opened the technical bids and checked them. Mainak did not assess the L&T proposal, and Parekh did not look into the WL Ross and Tech Mahindra bids due to a potential conflict of interest. HDFC, of which he was chairman, had a business link with the former, and he was a board member in Mahindra & Mahindra.

In the technical evaluation, the board cleared all three bidders for the financial round.

At 11.15 a.m., each bidder's representatives were invited and told they had qualified for the next round. The time had come for the financial bids to be opened by Chairman Karnik and Justice Bharucha in everybody's presence.

Justice Bharucha picked L&T's cover. When the seal was broken, and the number called out, I heaved a sigh of relief. He had read, '₹45.90.'

We held our collective breath as India's former Chief Justice got ready to unveil Tech Mahindra's offer. If it were anywhere between ₹43.2 and ₹52.8, we could see open bidding of the type you see in IPL.

Bharucha read out the number: '₹58.' That was 33 per cent above the average price since 7 January 2009! The professor who had made the prediction had struck gold.

Finally came WL Ross's quote. It showed ₹20. I was frankly disappointed. The price was approximately 60 per cent less than the previous day's market price of ₹48.

Tech Mahindra's was the highest bid, and the next best was below 90 per cent of this offer. Therefore, there was no need for an open auction. We verified the source of money for supporting the price quoted. The confirmation came soon.

Tech Mahindra was declared the winner. Manoj Bhat,

representing Tech Mahindra, along with Jatin Berry of Kotak Mahindra, was smiling.

By 12.45 p.m., three-and-half hours after the deadline for bidding expired, it was all over. An auction, which we expected would take up all day, had been quickly completed. It didn't bother us. What mattered is that we had found our suitor. Tech Mahindra would be the new owners. Of course, we had this little formality of the name being approved by the CLB.

Now was time for thanksgiving. The board thanked Justice Bharucha for his thoughtful guidance, appreciated the spectacular job done by the investment bankers Goldman Sachs and Avendus Capital Services, and recorded its gratitude for the invaluable services rendered by Homi Khusrokhan and Partho Datta. The board gave a thumbs-up for the commendable contribution of the dedicated team of Amarchand & Mangaldas & Suresh A. Shroff & Co., especially the husband and wife team of Shardul and Pallavi Shroff.

Somebody passed on a slip to me. 'A year ago, Satyam traded at ₹542 a share. Now Tech-M bought them for ₹58, at just 10 per cent of the price.' I thought that instead of assuming the purchase came at one-tenth of its value, let's believe the Satyam share once quoted 10 times its current value based on inflated results.

Was I happy with the way the bid price panned out?

My reasoning was as follows. Satyam was worth ₹150 per share. I was willing to take a ₹50 discount to compensate the buyer to meet unknown claims and class-action suits. I was ready to consider another ₹30 discount to pay them for the cost, untiring effort and the time they needed to clean up legacy issues. This brought the value down to ₹70. Thus, when the highest bidder quoted ₹58, I felt happy for Satyam. Perhaps, ₹12 (₹70–58) was about 20 per cent cushion Tech Mahindra kept if it came down to the slog overs of an open auction. I would not know because I never asked them.

To us, what this meant was Tech Mahindra would infuse capital of ₹2,889 crore and take over the company. Based on the bid price, the market capitalization of Satyam's expanded equity base would be about ₹5,600 crore (₹56 billion). At its peak, the firm's market capitalization stood at ₹36,600 crore (₹366 billion). The valuation had fallen to ₹404 crore (₹4.04 billion) based on the ₹6.30 share price. The price had now climbed 14 times in 100 days.[1]

That afternoon we addressed the media.

In the evening, we had a Leaders Call, and I took it while travelling in the car towards the airport. Some were jubilant at the development; others sounded curious if the merger would work out. Kiran and I assured them it would and was the best thing to happen.

◆

Appreciations started flowing in. The international media looked at the story as a unique case study of turnaround. Not many turnarounds have had a public–private partnership, with no infusion of taxpayer's money.

NASSCOM President Som Mittal, the first man to meet the grieving Satyam team, was generous. 'Everybody has worked to the moment. The government has acted on time to appoint a board, while the industry maintained restraint in not poaching the clients and employees of Satyam.'[2]

I rang up Y.H. Malegam and Venugopal C. Govind, two towering personalities in the accounting profession, to thank them for the guidance they offered me whenever I needed it during those 100 days. I spoke to Nestlé, who had volunteered

---

[1] 'Satyam Goes for Just One-tenth of Pre-Scam Price', *The Economic Times*, 13 April 2009, https://bit.ly/3oAERxW. Accessed on 26 July 2022.

[2] 'Tech Mahindra Wins Satyam Bid', *Firstpost*, 13 April 2009, https://bit.ly/3b40y6y. Accessed on 26 July 2022.

to be our ambassadors during those trying times. They were delighted at the call and reassured me they would continue with their support.

Two days later, on 15 April, I went to the Mayfair office. I sat with the finance team to authorize payment to service providers, including law firms, internal auditors, etc. A team member asked, 'You are making payments for services rendered to many people. What is in this for you?'

I said, 'What more can I ask for than the invaluable experience and the smiles on the faces of Satyamites and their families? Can anything be more valuable?'

On 16 April, the CLB approved Tech Mahindra's ₹58-a-share offer, saying it believed the new owner would nurture the company back to health. The CLB chairman recorded, 'Having convinced myself that the Board of Directors has selected a technically and financially competent/qualified strategic investor-M/s Venturbay-to adopt and nurture the ailing Satyam, I accept the recommendation to induct M/s Venturbay as the strategic investor.' It was very unusual for a quasi-judicial body to single out the board for having 'acted not only as directors but also like foster fathers to heal the wounds of the orphaned Satyam'.[3]

7 January to 16 April 2009, both days inclusive, marked 100 days of the revival task!

Tech Mahindra deposited in separate escrow accounts ₹1,756 crore, the subscription amount for a 31 per cent stake in the company's equity and ₹1,154 crore, the money needed to buy a 20 per cent stake in the open market.

On 20 April, Anand Mahindra first visited Satyam in Hyderabad. An alumnus of Harvard Business School, Anand would later, in 2020, be decorated with the Padma Bhushan. He

---

[3]'EX-99.2 CLB ORDER Dated April 16, 2009', SEC, https://bit.ly/3BiBt2p. Accessed on 26 July 2022.

appreciated the talented Satyamites who had kept the ship afloat amid turbulent weather. He congratulated the government-nominated board for saving the company. Satyamites were in tears of joy and expressed their gratitude to the 55-year-old billionaire businessman with a thank you card for taking over the company.

In the card, they wrote, 'Today marks a new beginning for both Satyam and Tech Mahindra. We thank you for your trust and your vision to see in Satyam what many couldn't: an opportunity to remake our industry and reach new levels of achievement and success. We're excited by this prospect and eager to work with you. We are confident that—together—we will succeed. Sincere thanks for your visit to Satyam. Satyam Team.'

Earlier, while the revival operation was on, I had analysed the nature of expenses and found scope for cost reduction. If implemented, Satyam could improve the bottom line considerably. The government-nominated board didn't have the time to implement all of them. At the dinner meeting at Hotel Novotel with Bharath Doshi, Group CFO of Mahindra & Mahindra, I shared these suggestions. His senior team members V.S. Parthasarathy, executive vice president of finance, M&A and IT, and S. Durgashankar, senior vice president, M&A, were also present.

For instance, the suggestions on the HR front included four measures. Rationalize the bench size to be in line with industry standards; rightsize the pyramid as the middle management appeared to be underutilized; trim at the top and empower the middle to shoulder those responsibilities, resulting in considerable savings. After all, 27 per cent of the associates took home 70 per cent of the salary package. And finally, add more workstations in owned premises and give up a few leased premises. Incidentally, Satyam had almost completed a new facility with 678 workspaces for occupation, I pointed out.

Where leased premises were retained, renegotiate rental on renewals using economic slowdown as an excuse and save costs.

In the days ahead, Satyam's 19 offices in Hyderabad were brought down to three locations through a judicious mix of adding workstations and centralizing places.

Due to pending approvals from antitrust authorities in Germany and the US, Tech Mahindra's nominees were not immediately co-opted to the board. Tech Mahindra nominated Ulhas N. Yargop, president, IT sector, Mahindra & Mahindra; Vineet Nayyar, vice chairman, managing director and CEO, Tech Mahindra; C.P. Gurnani, president, International Operations, Tech Mahindra; and Sanjay Kalra, president, Strategic Initiatives, Tech Mahindra. They were inducted into the board effective from 27 May that year. Nayyar was named whole-time director from 1 June 2009 and Gurnani became whole-time director and CEO, effective 23 June 2009. Simultaneously, S. Durgashankar took charge as CFO, and G. Jayaraman continued as company secretary.

India went to the polls with the first phase opening on 16 April and the last closing on 13 May. Three days later, on 16 May, the results were to be declared. In the small in-between window, on 14 May, Dr Manmohan Singh met us over tea at his residence at 7, Race Course Road, New Delhi. He had warm words of appreciation for our taking care of the nation's interests and upholding its image internationally.

On 17 July, the CLB passed an order allowing the MCA to withdraw four of the six directors nominated on the board of Satyam. Accordingly, Kiran, Deepak, Tarun and Mainak ceased to be the directors with effect from that day. Achuthan and I continued.

In that order, the CLB wrote: 'I convey my compliments and appreciation to these six nominee directors for their exemplary leadership during the troubled time, which enabled/ensured the stabilization of the company and also the smooth transition of the control of the company to the strategic investor.'

Even as we heaved a sigh of relief, stray comments were heard in the media. Would the merger work? Wouldn't we see a clash of cultures? Mahindra came from the staid ancient world of manufacturing, while Satyam was essentially a new-age company. Tech Mahindra was incorporated in 1986 as a joint venture between Mahindra Group and British Telecom and went public in August 2006.

In hindsight, the Mahindra takeover was ideal. For one, the Mahindras brought in the sharper processes you associate with the manufacturing industry. For another, if any of the technology industry titans had taken over Satyam, we would have seen large-scale retrenchment due to overlapping businesses. It's also not easy to work with people with whom you competed bitterly till the other day. In contrast, Tech Mahindra, with a single vertical, could now have a diversified portfolio and synergize smoothly without any disruption.

To put things in perspective, the government-nominated board held 16 meetings during its 100-day stint. Two of these meetings were spread over two days. In a typical scenario, a corporate holds four board meetings in a year. As company secretary, Jayaraman says, tongue-firmly-in-cheek, 'What ought to have been carried over four years has been held in a span of just 100 days.'

◆

SATYAM BIDDING PROCESS START TO FINISH (ALL IN 2009)

Serial No.	Events in Bidding Process	The Actual Dates
1	Public announcement on process inviting interested parties to register their interest	9 March
2	Interested bidders register	12 March, by 5 p.m.
3	RFP sent to interested bidders	13 March
4	Receive EOI from interested bidders along with proof of funds for ₹1,500 crore	20 March, by 5 p.m.
5	Board meeting to discuss EOIs and pre-qualification of bidders and final sign-off on information package and management presentation	21 March
6	Pre-qualification of bidders a. Intimation to bidders b. Submission of performance guarantee for ₹100 crore by bidders	23 March 27 March
7	Due diligence process a. Provide information package/access to the data room to pre-qualified bidders b. Provide draft share subscription agreement ('SSA') c. Pre-approved and monitored management presentation and access to company's legal advisors and finance team	25 March–12 April
8	Bidders submit technical and financial bids. Approval and signing of final SSA and declaration of successful bidder by the board	13 April
9	Submit a petition to CLB for the preferential allotment of shares	15 April
10	CLB approves Tech Mahindra (Venturbay) as the successful bidder and the allotment of shares subject to deposit of amount in an escrow account	16 April
11	Deposit of the amount towards 31 per cent preferential allotment and towards 20 per cent public offer in an escrow account	20 April
12	Tech Mahindra makes public offer	22 April

13	Preferential allotment of shares	5 May
14	New management/board induction	27 May
15	Withdrawal of special directors by government a. Four directors b. Two directors	17 July 2009 16 July 2012

PART 7

TAKEAWAYS

16

LEGISLATION AND GOVERNANCE

What are the lessons we can take away from the affairs of Satyam? There are meaningful ones for lawmakers and regulators from the perspective of enacting laws. We also have lessons for corporate entities from a governance perspective.

LESSON 1: REPAIR, DON'T REPLACE

In the celebrations that followed Satyam's revival, several debates took place on corporate governance in business and professional forums. Only in the previous year, Satyam had won the Golden Peacock Award for Corporate Excellence. The irony was striking. One school of thought was that if India wanted to halt Satyam's recurrence, regulators such as SEBI needed to plug the loopholes in the regulatory rules and guidelines. Another school felt the existing laws must be totally revamped by the lawmakers, the entire fabric of corporate regulation must be replaced to tighten governance and regulators must have more power to draw disclosure norms.

I agree with the first group. With every significant violation, we can fine-tune the law based on lessons learnt instead of making a drastic recast of the regulation. The legal luminary, Nani Palkhivala, would always say that it is better to iron out the creases instead of changing the entire fabric. First, we must understand that Satyam is an exception, not the rule. It's an aberration, not business-as-usual. You don't need to amend the Indian Penal Code with every murder.

At this point, I must tell you a story from Mayan mythology.

LESSON 2: PENULTIMATE PREPAREDNESS

In Mayan mythology, the world was destroyed four times. Every time, the Mayans learnt their lesson and vowed to be better protected from that particular menace. A flood destroyed the world on the first occasion. So, the survivors moved to higher ground well into the woods and put their houses on trees.

The next time, it was a fire that destroyed the world, and the Mayans' efforts went in vain. After that, the survivors built new homes out of stone. Soon enough, an earthquake destroyed the world. I can't recall the fourth destructive thing that happened, but whatever it was, I'm sure the Mayans were busy building shelters for the next earthquake.

This is called 'penultimate preparedness'. It is our way of making up for the fact that we didn't see the last thing coming along in the first place. However, we must carry out a risk assessment with foresight rather than hindsight and place checks and balances. And this applies to the prevention of fraud as well.

LESSON 3: LEGISLATING FOR THE EXCEPTION

If laws were to be made stringent to curb every offense, two undesirable fallouts would occur. First, the law would get further complicated, and two, the cost of compliance would go up significantly.

When the MCA wanted my suggestions for amending company law in the aftermath of Satyam, I not only provided insights but also gave them a caveat. I said, 'legislating for the exception' must be cautiously done. If we go overboard, the objective of keeping the law simple will be defeated. While there is room for improving the rules, there is no case for a drastic overhaul of the Companies Act, 1956, and SEBI Listing Obligations and Disclosure Requirements (LODR), making compliance difficult for genuine players. I pointed out that the Sarbanes-Oxley Act in the US, introduced in 2002, was diluted a few years later because companies became uncomfortable with excessive compliance requirements.

This reminds me of an oft-quoted story.

There was a train accident, and a commission was constituted to investigate it. The accident occurred due to the train derailing, travelling about 100 metres into a paddy field. It finally managed to stop but several passengers were injured by then. When the driver was examined, he said, 'A man suddenly appeared on the track, maybe to commit suicide.'

The furious commissioner asked, 'Don't you know the life of a stranger is insignificant compared to the safety of hundreds of passengers you were carrying? You should have run over him.'

The train driver didn't bat an eyelid. 'Do you think with 35 years of experience, I would be ignorant that that is what needs to be done? I wanted to run over him, but the guy started running into the paddy field, so I followed him.'

This is what happens in legislating for the exception. Just because someone abuses the law, the law is made more rigid for everyone. Introduced in the US after the catastrophic fall of Enron, did the Sarbanes-Oxley Act stop frauds like Xerox, WorldCom and Madoff? The answer is a resounding 'No'.

On the other hand, Madoff was a $65 billion fraud, and the promoter was imprisoned for 150 years by completing the trial within a year. This sent a strong signal to anyone aspiring to commit fraud. Therefore, quick investigation, expeditious trial and stringent punishment would prove a more effective deterrent than tighter laws, which become an inconvenience for everyone.

LESSON 4: EXPEDITIOUS ENFORCEMENT AND JUSTICE

A review of norms and laws is an ongoing process. The key to this is to strengthen enforcement. In India, cases drag interminably. Justice delayed is justice denied. The victims are frustrated at the delay in punishing the wrongdoer, and the accused is enraged that when he is acquitted, it is often too late.

Delayed justice also sends a weak signal to others to desist from committing fraud. A quick investigation, prompt filing of charges, expeditious trial, rapid judgment and exemplary punishment is far better than tinkering with the law. Most scams do not occur due to a lacuna in law but happen because there is a tendency to believe that one can do anything and get away with it. Even if caught, proceedings can be dragged and diluted over some time.

In addition to this, we need a speedy justice-delivery mechanism. India must revamp the entire judicial machinery to ensure that justice is carried out expeditiously.

Take the case of Satyam. All the issues we encountered overseas, such as the Upaid litigation, class-action suits, SEC violations, etc., were smoothly resolved within a year. In contrast, Satyam-related litigations in India are pending and have not been finally decided. Almost a decade has gone by, and we still have no light at the end of the tunnel.

If India has to become a developed economy and a global power, this scenario must change for good.

LESSON 5: BUILD QUALITY TEAMS AND DESIGN SUCCESSION PLANS

In an insider corporate governance model, the interactions are defined by both formal and informal rules and are largely relationship based. In contrast, in the outsider model, interactions are transactional, and shareholders and management may have divergent goals. In India, several companies follow the 'insider model' in running the company. Many developed economies have adopted the 'outsider model,' thereby enabling division of ownership and management. Creating independent professional teams at every level in an organization's hierarchy facilitates qualitative administration. Likewise, building professional teams for each vertical with a laid-down process creates a strong foundation for people's development.

The best thing Raju did was to build a multilayer leadership in the hierarchy. Even if the top leadership disappeared overnight, a clear definition of who would be next in command was in place—not just defined but also trained. A second- and a third-line leadership were nurtured to lead. There was no dearth of talent because a considerable amount was budgeted for imparting training. The spending was perceived as an investment and not an expenditure. Satyam survived the crisis only because the company had an excellent pool of people who ensured sustained operations. If Satyam had not done that, the revival would have proved to be a more Herculean task.

LESSON 6: FOCUS ON INTANGIBLES

While you must achieve impressive growth in sales, strengthen your asset base, improve profits and enhance market capitalization, these must not be done at the cost of compromising ethics. Over time, corporates have realized this—that too much emphasis on acquiring tangibles can be detrimental. In fact, it can be fatal if these come at the cost of values and principles.

Let us say an organization focusses more on intangibles such as goodwill, customer satisfaction, HR development, quality control, brand building, image and reputation, adherence to delivery, and contribution to social causes. Such a company will gradually rise from being a good company to a great company.

Over time, it will excel in its sector by setting best practices, getting emulated and respected across companies, and finally, emerging to be a role model in the corporate sphere.

This, in turn, will result in increased business and bring in tangible financial results. Impeccable adherence to values will lead to impressive economic performance. Tangibles are a corollary of intangibles. Devoid of a value-based approach, one cannot sustain business growth, reputation and accomplishment.

Satyam adhered to value systems on operational matters but faulted in falsifying accounts. That it was able to revive was due to the strong foundations built on intangibles.

◆

LEGAL AND REGULATORY CHANGES

Against the backdrop of the Satyam, Saradha and Sahara financial scandals, the new Companies Act of 2013 saw significant changes from the previous legislation of 1956. Similarly, SEBI brought in several changes in the corporate governance framework by way of amendment to the listing agreement. Subsequently, SEBI notified the LODR regulations in 2015, bringing in sweeping changes in the corporate governance framework. Both the MCA and SEBI modify certain provisions of the Companies Act, 2013, and LODR, respectively, from time to time to ensure that governance norms are robust and stakeholders' interest is protected.

SIGNIFICANT CHANGES IN COMPANY LAW

1. Section 118: Every company shall observe secretarial standards with respect to general and board meetings.
2. Section 125: The underlying shares of an unclaimed dividend lying for seven years shall also be transferred to the Investor Education Protection Fund (IEPF). That right of an investor over an unclaimed dividend or any unclaimed benefit from a security will not be extinguished.
3. Section 129: There must be compulsory consolidation of accounts of holding and subsidiary companies.
4. Section 132: The National Financial Reporting Authority (NFRA) has been given wider authority covering oversight and disciplinary mechanism of auditors. NFRA will also set audit standards.
5. Section 134: The scope of the Director's Responsibility Statement, to be part of the report of the board of directors to the shareholders, is enhanced to cover internal controls over financial reporting and establishment of proper systems to ensure compliance with all applicable laws.
6. Section 135: Qualifying companies each year shall ensure CSR spending of 2 per cent of the average net profits the company made during the three preceding financial years.
7. Section 138: Every listed company and a certain class of public and private companies must carry out an internal audit.
8. Section 139: There must be rotation of auditors after a specified time period introduced.

9. Section 143: Auditors, cost accountants or company secretaries of the company must inform fraud to the central government within the prescribed time and manner.
10. Section 147(5): The audit partner and the audit firm are jointly and severally liable for lapses in the discharge of audit function.
11. Section 149: Prescribed companies shall have a woman director.
12. Section 149: A listed public company shall have at least one-third of the total number of directors as independent directors, and their term shall not exceed five years. No such person can be appointed consecutively for more than two such terms.
13. Section 149(8): The Code for Independent Directors is laid out in Schedule IV of the Companies Act, 2013.
14. Section 165: The number of companies in which a person can be a director is restricted to 20, of which not more than 10 can be of public companies.
15. Section 177: Role and responsibility of audit committee widened including oversight on related party transactions.
16. Section 177(9): A certain category of companies must have a vigil mechanism for the directors and employees to report any unethical behaviour or other genuine concerns.
17. Section 178: Certain companies shall set up Nomination and Remuneration Committee (NRC), which shall decide the selection criteria, framing policy for appointment of directors and remuneration to directors and senior management for recommendation to the board. The committee shall also carry out evaluation of the performance of the directors.
18. Section 186: Investments are not to be made through more than two layers of investment companies.
19. Section 197(7): An independent director shall not be entitled to any remuneration other than sitting fee, reimbursement of expenses and profit-related commission. Independent director shall not be eligible to receive stock options.
20. Section 203: It is compulsory for certain companies to appoint (i) managing director or CEO or manager and in their absence a whole-time director, (ii) company secretary and (iii) CFO.
21. Section 204: Secretarial audit by a company secretary in practice is mandated for listed companies.
22. Section 211: Serious Fraud Investigation Office (SFIO) has been given a statutory recognition.

23. Section 212(8): SFIO has been conferred with the power to make arrests.
24. Section 245: A class-action suit can be filed by a prescribed number of members or depositors or a class of them.
25. Clause (4) under IV. Manner of appointment in Schedule IV: There must be compulsory issue of appointment letters to the non-executive directors and independent directors along with their roles and responsibilities, ethics, remuneration, etc.

SELECT CHANGES IN SEBI RULES AND REGULATIONS

26. Any pledging of shares by the promoters must be disclosed to the regulator.
27. Quality review has been introduced for audit firms eligible to audit listed entities.
28. Introduction of evaluation of the performance of independent directors and the board.
29. A person cannot be a director in more than seven listed entities, and a person who is a managing director cannot serve as an independent director in more than three listed entities.
30. Boards of top 1,000 listed companies must have at least one independent woman director. For any director above 75 years of age, in order to continue on the board, would require a special resolution of the shareholders.
31. The constitution of a Risk Management Committee is compulsory.
32. Senior management appointment and remuneration must be reviewed by the NRC.
33. There must be a review of the utilization of loans and advances of subsidiaries by the audit committee of the parent company.
34. On Related Party Transactions (RPTs), regulations now provide for omnibus approval, prior approval by the audit committee, material RPTs requiring shareholder approval, disclosure of half-yearly RPTs to stock exchanges, etc.
35. All listed companies must adopt a whistle-blower policy for employees and directors. In exceptional cases, provide direct access to the audit committee chairman.
36. Secretarial audit of a material unlisted Indian subsidiary is mandatory.
37. Independent director of the holding company shall be appointed as a director of the material subsidiary company.
38. The annual report is required to contain a matrix setting out the

competencies/expertise that the board believes its directors should possess.
39. There must be a Business Responsibility Report disclosing sustainability initiatives taken by the company, applicable to the top 1,000 listed entities.
40. Disclosure of initiation of forensic audit and final audit report by listed entities to the stock exchanges.

DECRIMINALIZATION OF COMPANY LAW

As feared, the Companies Act, 2013, turned out to be draconian, but following repeated representations, the government decriminalized several offenses over a period of time, which were reflected in the recommendations of the Company Law Committee, incorporated in the Companies (Amendment) Act, 2020.[1] This would enable the corporatization of partnership firms, boost the morale of companies operating in India and accelerate foreign investments. The idea is to reduce the judicial burden in proving the offenses and to enable expeditious closure of proceedings. The recommendations of the Company Law Committee, incorporated in the Companies (Amendment) Act, 2020, can be summarized as follows:

1. Re-categorization of 23 compoundable offenses to the In-house Adjudication Mechanism (IAM). Instead of court proceedings, the IAMs will determine penalties for these civil offenses.
2. The omission of seven compoundable offenses, which have a remedy under other law. For instance, non-compliance by company liquidators to be dealt with under the Insolvency & Bankruptcy Code, 2016 (IBC).
3. Limiting 11 compoundable offenses to levy of fines.
4. Providing an alternative framework for five offenses; for example, non-cooperation with the company liquidator by the promoter or director can be dealt with under IBC.
5. Lower penalties for certain offenses such as violations by one-person companies, small companies, start-ups, producer companies or by any of its officers in default.

---

[1]Chitravanshi, Ruchika, 'Government Decriminalises Companies Act to Promote Greater Ease of Doing Business', *Business Standard*, 21 September 2020, https://bit.ly/3vvZi3c. Accessed on 1 August 2022.

17
LEARNINGS FOR LIFE

My experiences at Satyam, during those momentous 100 days, taught me several moral lessons useful for life. Not that we don't know them. We are taught these from childhood. But some people lose sight of them, and some bury them deep so that they rarely surface, while others alienate them in their race for materialistic pursuits.

I wish to narrate them, one by one, connecting with my experience in Satyam's revival.

1. EGO HURTS; HUMILITY HELPS

The celebrated author, Ayn Rand, famously wrote that ego is the fountainhead of all progress. But in today's world, being humble and not headstrong can take you places.

In life, what we become depends on three elements: our thoughts, our intentions and our actions. Often, we have an exaggerated view of our strengths. When a task is accomplished, we think it is because of us and believe it could not have happened without us. This is the onset of ego, which enhances the feeling 'I am mighty, capable, intelligent and superior to others'.

No one can object to your believing, 'I can do this.' That is self-confidence. But to assert, 'I alone can do it' shows arrogance, arising out of ego. Remember, 'EGO' expands to 'Edging God Out'. Each one of us has a particular divinity within us. If we edge the deity out, we begin to think, 'I am solely responsible for what I achieved.' Many egoists disguise this as self-respect and therefore do not realize its ill effects. However, if we consider ourselves lucky enough to be the chosen one for the task and believe our Creator gives us the strength to execute it, the script changes. This approach inculcates humility in us. If something good happens, we feel happy. If it does not, we take it on the chin and proceed along with undiminished enthusiasm. This exorcises the 'I-Me-My-Mine' syndrome from us. Humility is the ability to give up one's pride while keeping one's dignity.

The way to grow without becoming egoistic is to use the head and heart appropriately. When success comes, do not let it get to your head. Do not become headstrong. Instead, take it to heart, celebrate and move on. On the contrary, when there is a setback, do not take it to heart and become depressed. Send it to your mind, analyse why it happened and then determine how to prevent its recurrence.

The Satyam proof

Several of Satyam's top brass shared with me their trauma following the dramatic events of 7 January. For many of them, the world collapsed. I found two classes of people among them. The first could take the shock with equanimity, while the second couldn't bite the bullet. The former regained their composure quickly because they had continually practised humility. They kept their head on their shoulders. The latter class was severely hit as they were used to wearing their ego on their sleeves.

In life, humility is the antidote to ego. Over time, the ego erodes the ability to empathize with others until we are placed in the same situation as others. Many associates realized this when Satyam erupted. Only now could they empathize with employees of Lehman Brothers!

The bottom line: With ego, you are gone; without it, you can go on.

2. ALWAYS EXPECT THE UNEXPECTED

Whatever will be, will be; the future is not for us to see. This is the meaning of the lyric *Que Sera, Sera*, immortalized in the 1950s song.

As the English writer Oscar Wilde wrote, 'To expect the unexpected shows a thoroughly modern intellect.' It means we must never take anything for granted and be prepared for the twists and turns of life. Towards that, always have a Plan B. This is not about being cynical but staying prepared for a possible gale storm. The phrase 'to expect the unexpected' can also mean positivity, of exceeding expectations. For example, you can get promoted when you least expect it!

Take challenging situations head-on, think outside the box and create new directions. Instead of blaming others for the setbacks, find out why things went wrong. If we acknowledge our mistakes, we can overcome disappointments and be freed from the fear of failure.

The 'expect the unexpected' philosophy leads to accepting that whatever will be will be. But at the same time, it reinforces a strong determination to face challenges in life. Those habituated to prepare for a rainy day were able to survive during the 2020 lockdown. Others found the going tough.

Some succeed, maybe because they are destined to succeed. But many succeed because they are determined to succeed. The former, destiny, is not in our hands; but the latter, determination, is very much in our control.

Cricket legend Sachin Tendulkar scored his ninety-ninth century on 12 March 2011. After that, in every innings he played, he wanted to hit his hundredth hundred, and his fans worldwide were waiting to celebrate. But it took the champion batsman 370 days and 34 innings to create history. On 16 March 2012, he scored the elusive hundredth ton in Dhaka against Bangladesh. If the man revered as the 'God of Cricket' had a 34-inning wait, we can't expect a cakewalk in our endeavours.

The Satyam proof

The events of 7 January 2009 made me introspect on this point. Imagine a well-qualified individual, endowed with unique skills, who works in a renowned company at a high pay. Imagine he suddenly finds his job is at stake, and the probability of receiving the coming month's salary is remote. He turns to his savings only to find the entire amount, once aggregating to a few crores, is now not worth the paper on which it is printed. They are ESOPs whose values have crashed. To top this, his daughter is of marriageable age.

It is a human tendency to hope that good times last forever. If we think of the possibility of bad times, someone will give advice to 'stay positive, ban negative thoughts'. 7 January 2009 taught everyone that the best course is to expect the unexpected and plan for a rainy day. It is not wrong to think of a glass half-filled with water as half-empty. Once in a while, we should ask ourselves how secure our family is financially. Ask yourself, 'Can my family and I lead an honourable everyday life if I stop earning from tomorrow?' Proper design of investments and periodic review protect us and act as a lifeboat.

Another point merits attention. Apart from securing your financial future, arm yourself with a transferable skill set so that when the winds of change blow, as they invariably will, you stay relevant in your organization. Even if the company gets blown over, you can always move on to another entity, which will take you in if you are well equipped.

The bottom line: Always plan for a rainy day.

3. DIFFERENTIATE BETWEEN OPPORTUNITIES AND TEMPTATIONS

'Opportunity knocks the door but once, while temptation leans on the doorbell forever,' wrote a famous author.

We must segregate the knock from the noise. It is easier to succumb to temptation than to make a calibrated attempt to reap the fruits of opportunities. For sure, all of us should aspire to do more in our life. However, many of us fall into traps of our own making. Three things lead to this fall: opportunity, temptation and willpower. Let me explain.

If you find a wallet on the road, you can either try and find the owner or tell yourself that the finders keepers. What you do defines you. When you have several such opportunities, you might get tempted. For example, if you regularly find lost wallets, you might be once tempted to think, 'Why not pocket it just this one time?' When you desperately want something, you become even more tempted to break the rules. It depends on our moral fibre and also on whether we think we will be caught and punished. If we believe we can get away with it, the temptation to succumb is greater. This is one reason why we usually jump traffic signals at night and abuse strangers on social media.

Whether we resist the temptation depends on our willpower. Willpower is about 'not doing what we know we should not do'. The will required is higher when the desire is strong, and the perceived risk is less. Willpower involves making a choice, including the decision on whether to give in to the temptation or not. Stay strong, and you will win in the long run.

Many lose their peace of mind by comparing themselves with others regarding fame, power, position, money and possessions. They fail to appreciate that just as those opportunities and skills vary from person to person, so do the outcomes. Generally, we overvalue what others possess and undervalue what we own. While contentment strengthens our willpower, greed breeds temptation. In life, happiness is bliss. If you are not contented, whatever be your wealth, you will always feel inadequate.

Have aspiration, but avoid greed. Aspiration makes life interesting, but greed can lead to destruction. There are two differences between aspiration and greed. The former is always accomplished through ethical means. The latter seeks to find shortcuts; its objective is to achieve the goal by hook or by crook. The second difference is that those who aspire feel happy when they win. If they lose, they accept it and move on. Even if they receive what they wanted, the greedy ones are never contented and want more. That ultimately leads to misery.

The Satyam proof

Ramalinga Raju had the opportunity to belong to the pantheon of the greats. He had no background in technology, unlike his peers in the Big Three—TCS, Infosys and Wipro—yet, he was in their midst in terms of his vision and effort. To do business in 66 countries worldwide and have 185 Fortune 500 companies as customers, you need extreme self-confidence, bordering on chutzpah. Raju had everything going his way. But instead of focussing on the opportunities, he succumbed to the temptation of fudging the numbers. In the end, Frankenstein's monster trapped him.

The bottom line: Character is more important than reputation because while character is what you really are, reputation is what others think you are.

4. EVERYONE IS ACCOUNTABLE TO THEIR OWN CONSCIENCE

Conscience is the still small voice of God that resides in man. It's a person's moral compass. Doing what you do when you are watched reflects on your conduct. Doing what you do when you are not monitored tests your character. When you follow the traffic rules while the traffic constable is around, it speaks of your good conduct. But if you follow the rules even when no one is around, it talks about your good character. Never think you are alone; we are watched continuously, as this story shows.

One evening, a guru gave an apple each to his three disciples and asked them to eat it when no one was watching them. A few hours later, the first disciple returned, saying he got into a well when dark, and no one saw him eat the apple. The second disciple turned up the following day, said he walked deep into the forest to sit behind the trees and chew. After a few days, the third disciple turned up with a sad face. When the guru asked, 'What happened?' he replied, 'I could not do what you told me because, wherever I went, I felt the presence of divine power.'

It means you are never alone, as God is always your supreme companion and omnipresent.

The Satyam proof

When Satyam first began cooking the books, the still small voice of inner conscience would have alerted Raju that he was doing something wrong. Indeed, he would have been perturbed. After all, only a good man could have created facilities like 108 and 104.

Raju had the option of playing straight. In that case, both the ranking and share price would have slipped. Normally, it should not have mattered because as long as you are ethical, you sleep peacefully. This alert from the conscience would have been there in the beginning. But with each passing quarter, the inner voice got silenced. Had he listened to his conscience, we would have had a completely different story today.

The bottom line: Listen to your inner voice. Do the right thing even if no one is watching.

5. ADAPT TO TRENDS IN KNOWLEDGE AND SKILLS, BUT STAY STATIC ON FUNDAMENTALS

The world is dynamic, and the way businesses are run changes with time. Technology has introduced us to a digital era. Demonetization facilitated online banking and reduced footfalls in bank branches. The pandemic has accelerated the forces of change, leading to innovative ideas such as work from home and digital classrooms. All these validate what Charles Darwin once said, 'It is not the strongest of the species that survives, nor the most intelligent, but rather the one most responsive to change.' To stay relevant, we must empower ourselves with new-age skills.

Remember that while everything, including lifestyles, change, the fundamental values of life remain constant. The same ethical values of the fifteenth century govern us in the twenty-first century and will continue to rule the world in the twenty-fifth century. Therefore, while we must adapt to a changing world, we must not let our guard slip when it comes to fair play. If we do so, it will be at our peril.

Indeed, you must flow like water in a stream in the quest for recent trends in technology, knowledge and skills but stand firm like a rock when it comes to the fundamentals of our lives.

The Satyam proof

Satyam's growth was rapid, primarily because it adapted to and embraced how the software industry was developing. Raju empowered thousands of youth with technological and other skills to excel in the field. Customer expectations were met and even surpassed with innovation and creativity.

For instance, in the 1990s, you had to pay a tax to use certain roads in Singapore. Initially, these were introduced with staffed booths. Satyam developed and installed the sensor system with prepaid cards. It helped collect taxes by remote sensing, thereby reducing the queue time at the booths. This transformation spread across the globe and is happening now in India in the highway tollbooths. While this proactive adaptability to innovative trends enabled Satyam to scale new heights, skipping the fundamental ethical values in accounting and reporting led to its downfall.

The bottom line: Like a tree sheds leaves and not its roots, we can change our views but not our values.

6. MANY GOOD DEEDS GET WASHED AWAY BY ONE BAD ACT

In accounting, every credit has a corresponding debit. Similarly, you cannot commit a crime in real life and say a good deed done in the past cancels it out. A negative plus a positive is, like in mathematics, still a negative. A zero multiplied with any significant number is always zero. Just as a drop of poison spoils the purity of an entire pot of milk, a single misdeed is enough to destroy goodwill built over a lifetime. Yes, all the perfumes of Arabia cannot take away the stench and stink of a single act.

The Satyam proof

Raju has innumerable good deeds to his credit. Establishing the Byrraju Foundation, setting up '108' under EMRI, empowering '104' under HMRI, creating world-class infrastructure at Satyam and nurturing a large talent pool—these are just a few things we have looked at. It takes several good deeds to build an excellent reputation and only one wrong move to lose it. Alas, the cooking of the books was the poison that destroyed this milk pot's purity. It takes years and several good deeds to build goodwill and the image of a person, but the whole thing can be wiped out by one act of crime or unethical behaviour. Building a reputation is like rolling up a rock to the top of a mountain, whereas losing credibility is like allowing the same rock to slip and tumble to the bottom. It takes immense effort to push the rock up, but one small push can send it hurtling down.

The bottom line: In life's book of accounts, you don't have contra entries. One credit doesn't compensate for a debit.

7. TO LEAVE FOOTPRINTS, LOVE PEOPLE, NOT WEALTH

With materialism ruling modern society, the thirst for accumulating wealth sees no boundaries. Siddhartha left his palace in the quest for peace and emerged as Gautama Buddha, the enlightened one. In contrast, many of us are in search of prosperity at the cost of peace. Often, we achieve many things that do not compensate for what we have lost in the bargain.

Alexander the Great established the largest empire the ancient world had ever seen as King of Macedonia and Persia. He once called his general and instructed him that when he (Alexander) died, his corpse be taken in procession along the streets with both hands dangling outside the coffin. When the general asked why, the King said, 'I want people to know that I came empty-handed into this world and likewise will go empty-handed from this world.'

In life, what keeps us afloat is empathy for people and the warmth we share with them. Life, by itself, has no meaning. It is for us to give life a purpose and justify our existence.

We learn during the first 25 years of our lives, and for the next 35, we earn. After that, we retire to enjoy the pleasures of the world until the day we take our final breath. This is our life in a nutshell. Isn't that tedious and monotonous? Life truly becomes meaningful when we share our knowledge and wealth with those who require them the most. This is what elevates our lives from being meaningless to leaving an impression in society. However, if we use knowledge and effort only to amass more wealth, we have not done much to make this world a better place.

So, instead of merely adding years to the life we live, let us add life to the years we live. The gentle footprints of kindness make soft imprints in the heart that will never be erased.

The Satyam proof

To a large extent, Raju gave meaning to life. His Byrraju Foundation, EMRI and HMRI initiatives were aimed at the larger good of his countrymen. How he changed people's lives in his native Andhra will live on in people's hearts. He will be remembered forever for his contribution to society, even if corporate India chooses to remember him for the accounting subterfuge. In the commercial world, good deeds are seldom remembered, but the bad ones are rarely forgotten.

The bottom line: True happiness comes not from having much to live on but from having much to live for.

8. ABILITY TAKES YOU TO THE TOP, BUT YOU NEED INTEGRITY TO STAY THERE

Many people start from scratch and yet scale great heights in life. They are the real 'slumdog millionaires'. It comes out of vision, hard work and competence. On the other hand, we see people at their peak experience a mighty fall. Analyse the situation and you will find that while anyone can build institutions through sweat, tears and toil, one requires an invincible character to maintain growth and stature.

Mahatma Gandhi said that the means justify the end. How you achieve your goal is as important as achieving the goal itself. Therefore, value must be kept at the highest row and must never be compromised, regardless of any situation.

Remember, unless we stand for something, we may fall for anything.

The Satyam proof

Building an organization from scratch is always an inspiring story. Satyam, which was founded in 1987, initially had calibrated growth. Who would have imagined that a 33-year-old could promote, nurture and grow a company with world-class infrastructure, manned by 51,000 employees, spread across 66 countries, catering to the needs of top-class MNCs? Except, of course, the man himself, B. Ramalinga Raju. This reinforced the philosophy that if you have self-confidence, you can conquer the world even if no one believes in you.

Raju could reach the top only due to his vision, hard work, innovation and creativity, all driven by a sense of competitiveness. Unfortunately, he compromised on his principles, thus opening the door to demolish what he built. Yes, ability takes you up the ladder, but it requires integrity to stay at the top.

The bottom line: Have integrity. No one gets lost on a straight road.

9. DO YOUR DUTY UNMINDFUL OF THE CONSEQUENCES

In the Kurukshetra war, Lord Krishna tells Arjuna to set his heart upon his work (karma) but never its rewards.

It is incredible what you can accomplish if you do not care who gets the credit. An ordinary mind is governed by the thought of 'What is in it for me (WIFM)'. But that approach does not take us anywhere. Even when one works for an organization, there must be a holistic approach to rank self-interest as the third in sequence after the organization's interest and team's interest. If we do that, our self-interest will be automatically taken care of, way beyond our expectations in the long run.

The Satyam proof

When we walked in to revive Satyam, our only objective was to redeem India's reputation in the eyes of global investors. We also wanted to protect the stakeholders' interests, including employees, shareholders and customers. I, personally, further envisioned repairing any damage inflicted on the CA profession due to the audit failure. I had nothing in mind for personal gain. Only due to this could I push myself in many trying circumstances. The Padma Shri came along the way, which I least expected.

The bottom line: Everyone's purpose in life is their life preserver.

10. ANYTHING IS POSSIBLE WITH GOOD INTENTIONS

Anything is possible if we set our heart and soul towards achieving it. What can be achieved is restricted only by what can be imagined. If you begin with the right intentions, you will reach the right destination. When you plunge into a challenging task for a significant cause with no personal interest, you get enormous inner energy to accomplish it.

'Impossible,' said Napoleon Bonaparte, 'is found in the dictionary of fools.' Someone quipped, Impossible itself says, 'I'm possible.'

Always train as if you are the worst, and play as if you are the best. When preparing for any task, you must be pessimistic and equip yourself for the worst-case scenario. Then, nothing will surprise you, as you will be ready for any situation. However, when you start executing something, you should be optimistic that you will excel at it. The one who invented the parachute looked at all possibilities while flying, but the inventor didn't look forward to using the parachute when he stepped into an aircraft.

The Satyam proof

When we, the government-nominated board of directors, started our mission, reviving Satyam looked impossible. There were disparaging comments and discouraging moments. Several times, we got depressed and frustrated at hitting a dead end. We had to muster all our inner energies to reassure ourselves that what appeared to be the end of the road was only a bend in the road. I kept reminding myself that the story of several failures is about those who gave up, not knowing how close they were to success.

It is the culture of crossing the finishing line even in the most adverse situation that stood by us.

Many customers who were keen on migrating to competitors changed their minds. They started to trust us when they learnt we were working pro bono. We believed the smiles on the associates' faces, and that of the family members and shareholders are more valuable than monetary benefits. Thanks to our right intentions and God's intervention at critical times, we could achieve the turnaround.

The bottom line: When you are working for a public cause, the whole universe conspires to help.

PERSONAL LESSONS: A QUICK RECAP

1. Humility helps. Ego hurts.
2. Expect the unexpected.
3. Differentiate between opportunities and temptations.
4. Everyone is accountable to their own conscience.
5. Adapt to trends in knowledge and skills, but stay static on fundamentals.
6. Many good acts are washed away by one bad act.
7. To leave a legacy, love people, not wealth.
8. Ability takes you to the top, but you need integrity to stay there.
9. Do your duty unmindful of the consequences.
10. Anything is possible with good intentions.

PART 8

THE DENOUEMENT

18

AWARD AND EPILOGUE

Dateline: 7 April 2010

Venue: Durbar Hall, Rashtrapati Bhavan, New Delhi

I got up from my seat the moment my name was called and began my walk towards the President of India. The previous day, we had a recce when we were told which way to proceed and how to return.

This hall was where India's first Indian governor general, C. Rajagopalachari, and India's first prime minister, Jawaharlal Nehru, took their oaths of office. Christopher Hussey, the historian, wrote, 'The impact of the Durbar Hall, however approached, is immediate, overwhelming, and utterly silencing.'[1] I could not agree more.

On 25 January 2010, on the eve of India's sixtieth Republic Day anniversary, the home ministry informed me that my name would be announced the following day as a 'Padma Shri' awardee. My first thought was, 'Why me?'

I was eager to know who recommended my name, and the caller said, 'The Satyam Board.'

The board's gesture and their doing so without letting me know about it moved me. At one level, I was excited. At the same time, I was a bit angry with the government. As a citizen,

---

[1]'Durbar Hall', Rashtrapati Bhavan, https://bit.ly/3oBi59r. Accessed on 27 July 2022.

I had done my duty and expected nothing in return, and here they were, settling it with an award. But the hurt vanished when, across India, the CA community, to whom I owe my rise in the public eye, feted me with unalloyed joy. They took the prize as recognition for the profession. At that point, I was happy to have added to the goodwill of the profession.

I remembered Tarun. Remember, 15 months ago, at a breakfast table at Novotel, I had turned down the offer of being designated the position of a whole-time director while agreeing to take up the responsibilities associated with the role. He had said, 'The world will not know your contribution.'

Tarun seemed to have had the last laugh. I learnt that he was instrumental in initiating my name through the board for the Padma award. This was his way of letting the world know about my work. What a fine human being!

I walked up to receive the award from the President of India as the Prime Minister and the audience that included my 80-year-old mother, Saradhammal, and my wife, Dr Sujatha, applauded. My daughters, Malavika and Sahini, watched on television in our Chennai home.

As I joined the palms of my hands in the traditional namaste, President Pratibha Patil, standing on the dais, handed over the citation and decorated me with the medal. I felt doubly blessed. 7 April was my fifty-fourth birthday, and I couldn't have asked for a better gift.

Two thousand three hundred kilometres away, in my native Rajakoil village, Gudiyatham, near Vellore in Tamil Nadu, my 95-year-old father, Narayanaswamy Chowdhry, now fully blind, was sitting in front of a television. My brother, T.N. Rajendran, and sister, Premalatha Chandrababu, were briefing him about the proceedings shown live on Doordarshan. My father, a Gandhian and a freedom fighter, was delighted when my name was announced. There was not a single dry eye in the room. How I wished he could also see.

My eldest brother Dr T.N. Gajendran and my eldest sister Aruna Subramanyam watched with their families in Chennai and Bengaluru.

Eleven years on, I think the evening at Rashtrapati Bhavan was an incredible moment in my life. The awardees that year included Saina Nehwal, Virender Sehwag, Narain Karthikeyan and Ramakant Achrekar for sports, actors Rekha and Saif Ali Khan for Art, Rajalakshmi Parthasarathy (best known as Mrs YGP) for education and Venu Srinivasan for trade and industry.

On 11 April 2009, two days before we found our new promoters, the Satyam leadership team took me to the Satyam Technology Center (STC) in Bahadurpally. In STC, there is a spot at the main entrance, where I was asked to stand. I slowly found others moving away, leaving me alone. Even as I stood puzzled, I felt rose petals being showered on me from the top and the leadership team applauding. I was stunned. The press of a button had engineered the dropping of the petals. They told me that in the past, this was done for a few exceptional dignitaries. They said they wanted to express their gratitude. I was moved by their gesture.

A few months later, in 2009, the Mahindra Satyam family presented me a portrait of mine drawn by a Satyamite's son Karthik with the following message:

> Dear Uncle, My daddy says you are the best uncle in the world. He told me the story of how you rescued us from big trouble. I have seen my dad worried about work, but now he is not worried any more. He loves going to office. We are proud of you. You must never forget us. Please take care of yourself and continue to love us always.

It was signed, 'Karthik, 9 years—A proud Satyamite!'

The portrait is even today wall-mounted in the Satyam Infocity campus with the sign-off: 'With the deepest gratitude—From the Mahindra Satyam Family.'

These few lines from Karthik resonated with the inscription on the Padma Award: 'I, President of India, Pratibha Devisingh Patil, am awarding you Padma Shri in honor of your personal qualities.'

Achuthan and I were happy to work with the new board. Many of the pending tasks were continued with zeal and completed. The loans raised from IDBI and BoB were fully repaid in May 2009 itself. The Upaid case was settled at $70 million. On 26 October 2009, the Satyam board received the 'Business leadership' award from NDTV Profit. We were honoured to receive it from Finance Minister Pranab Mukherjee at Taj Lands End, Mumbai. Shri Mukherjee would later become India's president.

Two months later, on 21 December, we got the CNN-IBN Indian of the Year Award under the Business category. Dr Manmohan Singh personally gave the award at Taj Palace, New Delhi.

♦

Meanwhile, in June 2009, Satyam was rechristened Mahindra Satyam. The Satyam brand was continued to ensure recognition in the marketplace. It was also one way of telling the world, 'Look, Satyam has been revived.' Forensic audit for the period beginning 1 April 2002 revealed a gap of ₹1,122 crore between the books and actuals. This was treated as part of the prior period item in the accounts for the year ended 31 March 2009. The shareholders at the Annual General Meeting held on 21 December 2010 adopted this.

Tech Mahindra decided to merge with Mahindra Satyam (M-Sat) with effect from 1 April 2011. The boards of the two companies gave the nod to proceed, and so did the regulatory bodies. Shareholders approved these in January 2013, and with that, the Satyam brand became history. The merger ran into some delay due to ambiguity over jurisdiction between investigating agencies and the government. On 11 June 2013, the Andhra Pradesh High Court approved the merger after the Bombay High Court demurred. Orders of both the high courts were delivered to the Registrar of Companies on 24 June 2013.

The merger was formally completed on 24 June 2013, creating India's fifth-largest software services company with a turnover of $2.7 billion. Anand Mahindra as chairman, Vineet Nayyar as executive vice chairman and C.P. Gurnani as the managing director were at the helm of affairs. So were Milind Kulkarni as CFO and G. Jayaraman as company secretary.

M-Sat shareholders received two shares of Tech Mahindra stock for every 17 shares of M-Sat they owned. The shares in the new entity began trading on 12 July 2013.

◆

The claim of ₹1,230 crore by the 37 Hyderabad-based agro-companies as loans given to Satyam, laid out in Raju's confession letter, is sub judice. These companies petitioned the City Civil Court, Secunderabad. One of these claims has been converted into a suit, and the rest are at various stages of admission.

When Satyam was being merged with Tech Mahindra, these companies approached the Andhra Pradesh High Court and opposed the merger. While approving the merger, the court held that in the absence of documentary evidence, the new management is justified in disclosing such payments as 'amounts pending investigation suspense account (net)' in the financial statements. Thus, this treatment has judicial backing.

The ED had initiated action under the Prevention of Money Laundering Act, 2002. It directed Satyam not to return the ₹1,230 crore, claiming that these are proceeds of crime. It also attached fixed deposits of ₹822 crore as 'proceeds of crime.' Tech Mahindra challenged the action before the Andhra Pradesh High Court. The court stayed the order. The ED filed a Special Leave Petition in the Supreme Court, which the Court dismissed on 26 February 2021.

The ED initiated criminal proceedings against the company along with Raju and others. The High Court quashed these proceedings against Tech Mahindra, and when the ED filed a Special Leave Petition, the apex court dismissed it. With these two decisions, the stigma of alleging money laundering and possession of proceeds of crime with Tech Mahindra stands settled.

On its part, the Income Tax Department raised a demand for ₹617 crore for financial years 2002–03 to 2006–07 by disallowing foreign tax credit, an exemption for export profits under Section 10A and a part of expenses.

Satyam had no quarrels with the procedure and suggested removing the fake turnover and fictitious interest income on non-existent fixed deposits. Satyam also requested an exemption for export profit and credit for foreign taxes paid after verifying their genuineness. This could lead to nullifying the demand and may even result in a refund. After all, the SFIO, CBI and forensic auditors had certified the amounts in question in their respective reports.

The Income Tax Department rejected the contention, arguing Satyam had on its own offered them as income. The company petitioned the Central Board of Direct Taxes (CBDT) to intervene and instruct the assessing officer to stay the demand. The CBDT refused. Satyam then moved the Andhra Pradesh High Court, which granted partial relief. Aggrieved, the company knocked at the doors of the Supreme Court on 14 April 2011. The apex court directed the CBDT to reconsider the matter after asking Satyam to furnish a ₹617 crore bank guarantee.

On reconsideration, the CBDT did not change its stand, and so the company preferred an appeal to the Andhra Pradesh High Court. The court ordered a stay of all proceedings.

Upon merger of Satyam with Tech Mahindra, consummated on 24 June 2013, Tech Mahindra stepped into the shoes of Satyam in pursuing the litigation and follow-up efforts. It has approached the CBDT to look into the matter on a holistic basis.

◆

In 2015, Ramalinga Raju, the man who had started the train of events that led us to get into the Satyam board, was sentenced to seven years in jail and fined ₹5.50 crore (then equivalent of $8,00,000) by the CBI court. He is out on bail, and the verdict has been challenged.

The auditors, too, faced legal sanctions. The engagement partner for the audit from PW for the period 2000–07 was S. Gopalakrishnan, and since then, till September 2008, the mantle fell on S. Talluri.

In May 2012, ICAI's Disciplinary Committee debarred both the auditors, who had signed the financial statements on behalf of PW, from practising for life. The Appellate Tribunal upheld the committee's decision in Gopalakrishnan's case, while the matter is pending disposal in Talluri's case. The Delhi High Court has admitted a writ petition filed by Gopalakrishnan against these verdicts in September 2015, which again is pending disposal.

In April 2015, the two auditors were convicted and sentenced by the CBI court. However, the sessions court suspended the sentence but is yet to dispose of the appeal.

In January 2018, SEBI debarred the PW network for two years from auditing listed entities besides disgorgement fees.

In September 2019, the Securities Appellate Tribunal (SAT), while upholding the order on disgorging the fee amount, quashed the order on debarring the firms in PW network and partners from auditing listed companies. SAT ruled that SEBI had no jurisdiction over the auditors as the latter could not prove whether the auditors participated in the fraud.

SEBI has challenged this order in the Supreme Court.

The company paid $125 million to settle class-action suits by the US shareholders.[2]

---

[2]'Mahindra Satyam Ends Its Litigations in US', *The Times of India*, 29 July 2012, https://bit.ly/3cKjaZZ. Accessed on 27 July 2022.

AWARD AND EPILOGUE

Shareholders who stayed with the company over these years have been richly rewarded. If they bought 1,700 shares at the bid price of ₹58 and valued at ₹98,600, they would have received a 1:1 bonus, a stock split that reduced the face value from ₹10 to ₹5, and a 2 for 17 swap when the merger took place. This would mean the shareholder would own 800 shares today. At a market price of ₹1,016 on 30 June 2022, the value of holding is ₹812,800 and translates into an 18 per cent compounded return per annum.

The merger helped Tech Mahindra go up the pecking order among technology companies. It was able to diversify its business, the profile of customers and the geographical spread. The very fact that many Satyam employees are today with Tech Mahindra is an indication that the merger has worked beyond anyone's wildest dreams. It's an indication of the synergy and convergence between the two firms.

As of 31 March 2022, Tech Mahindra Limited is a $5.998 billion (Previous Year $5.111 billion) entity with 1,224 clients, and is home to 151,173 employees across 90 countries. It continues to be fifth in the Indian IT sweepstakes.

Deepak Parekh continues to be the chairman of HDFC. Kiran Karnik sits on the governing body of HelpAge India. Tarun Das chairs the Institute of Economic Growth. S. Balakrishna Mainak rose to become the managing director of LIC and has since retired. C. Achuthan did a remarkable job as chairman of the Takeover Regulations Advisory Committee, constituted by SEBI, and submitted his report on 19 July 2010. Unfortunately, he passed away while on his way to Sabarimala in 2011. He was 70. I miss the warm welcome he would accord to me in his office whenever I visited Mumbai.

I became chairman of Canara Bank and held that position for five years before stepping down in August 2020. I assumed office as chairman of IDBI from 9 May 2022. I sit on the boards of Mahindra & Mahindra and National Bank for Financing

Infrastructure and Development (NaBFID) as independent director. I continue to be on the board of Tech Mahindra.

It is a matter of pride for me to have been part of the most incredible rescue operation in corporate history.

ACKNOWLEDGEMENTS

We would like to thank the following people:

- Usha Natarajan, for helping in preparing the manuscript
- D. Theresa, Janani Venkatesan, Jeby George, K.R. Srivats, R. Varun, T.M. Malavika, Ramya Venkat and Sahini Manoharan for providing valuable inputs to the manuscript
- Narayan Shankar, Anil Khatri and Raji Reddy, for vetting the 'Corporate Lessons'
- G. Jayaraman and V. Murali, for providing insights from the Satyam perspective
- Manoj Bhat and Milind Kulkarni, for vetting the manuscript from the Tech Mahindra perspective
- M. Sivakumar, for being our first critic
- Malaiselvan Nagarajan, for designing and layout of the manuscript
- Yaminini Chowdhury, for reaching out to us for the book
- Kanishka Gupta, for representing us before Rupa Publications
- Aurodeep Mukherjee and Manali Das, for editing the manuscript

LIST OF ABBREVIATIONS

ADMS	Application Development, Maintenance and Support
APIIC	Andhra Pradesh Industrial Infrastructure Corporation
BCG	Boston Consulting Group
BMI	Bank Muscat International
BoB	Bank of Baroda
BPO	Business Process Outsourcing
BSE	Bombay Stock Exchange
CA	Chartered Accountant
CB-CID	Crime Branch-Criminal Investigation Department
CBDT	Central Board of Direct Taxes
CBI	Central Bureau of Investigation
CEO	Chief Executive Officer
CFO	Chief Financial Officer
CII	Confederation of Indian Industry
CLB	Company Law Board
COO	Chief Operating Officer
CSR	Corporate Social Responsibility
ED	Directorate of Enforcement
EMRI	Emergency Management and Research Institute
EOI	Expression of Interest
ESOPs	Employee Stock Option Plans
ERP	Enterprise Resource Planning
HMRI	Health Management and Research Institute
HR	Human Resources

LIST OF ABBREVIATIONS

IAM	In-house Adjudication Mechanism
IAS	Indian Administrative Service
IBC	Insolvency & Bankruptcy Code, 2016
ICAI	Institute of Chartered Accountants of India
IIM	Indian Institute of Management
IIT	Indian Institute of Technology
IP	Intellectual property
IPL	Indian Premier League
ISB	Indian School of Business
IST	Indian Standard Time
IT	Information Technology
L&T	Larsen & Toubro
LIC	Life Insurance Corporation of India
LODR	Listing Obligations and Disclosure Requirements
M&A	Merger & Acquisition
M-Sat	Mahindra Satyam
MCA	Ministry of Corporate Affairs
MNC	Multinational Corporations
MoU	Memorandum of Understanding
NAB	National Australian Bank
NASSCOM	National Association of Software and Service Companies
NFRA	National Financial Reporting Authority
NRC	Nomination and Remuneration Committee
NSE	National Stock Exchange
NYSE	New York Stock Exchange
PE	Private Equity
PF	Provident Fund
PMO	Prime Minister's Office
PW	Price Waterhouse
RBI	Reserve Bank of India
RFP	Request for Proposal
RoC	Registrar of Companies

RPT	Related Party Transactions
SAT	Securities Appellate Tribunal
SEBI	Securities and Exchange Board of India
SEC	US Securities and Exchange Commission
SEZ	Special Economic Zone
SFIO	Serious Fraud Investigation Office
SLC	Satyam Learning Center
SSA	Share Subscription Agreement
SSL	Satyam School of Leadership
STC	Satyam Technology Center
STP	Software Technology Park
TDS	Tax Deducted at Source

INDEX

108 Service, 67

Abdul Kalam, A.P.J., Dr, 71
Abercrombie & Fitch, 136
Achuthan, C., xxi, 7, 19, 20, 21, 32, 116, 170, 172, 219
Advani, L.K., xxv
Ajman government, 140
Alexander the Great, 204
Andersen, Arthur, 138
Andhra Pradesh Industrial Infrastructure Corporation, 88, 148, 149
Arjuna, 206
asset stripping, 162
Avendus, 88, 90, 154, 159, 170, 175

Bahadurpally, 12, 31, 109, 213
Bainbridge, Andrew, 96
Bank Muscat International (BMI), 96, 97, 99
Bank of Baroda (BoB), 84, 88, 91, 100, 115, 146, 148, 149, 150, 215
Batelco, 97, 99
Berry, Jatin, 170
Bharat Sanchar Nigam Limited, 103
Bharucha, Sam Piroj, 155
Bhat, Manoj, 170, 174, 221
bid process letter, 163

BNP Paribas, 40, 41, 91
Bombardier, 136
Bombay High Court, 215
Boston Consulting Group (BCG), 89, 101, 137, 138, 157
Brahmayya & Co, 39, 77
'Breaking News', 131
Bright, Craig, 142
British Telecom, 180
Bush government, 10
Byrraju Foundation, 65, 203, 205

cash and bank balance, 53, 55, 58
Changavalli, Venkat, 72
Chhatrapati Shivaji Terminus, xxv
Chief Justice of India, 155
CISCO Systems, 136
Citibank, 40, 91, 148
clash of cultures, 180
class-action suits, 11, 59, 80, 89, 122, 163, 175, 188, 218
Clinton, Bill, 4, 138
closed bidding, 164
Coca-Cola, 79, 136
Cognizant, 163, 165, 173
Colaba, xxv, 166
commercial taxes department, 91, 119
Companies Act, 1956, 21, 86, 155, 187
Company Law Board (CLB), 21,

33, 34, 35, 85, 86, 91, 92, 93,
115, 123, 154, 155, 157, 159,
175, 177, 179, 181
Confederation of Indian Industry
(CII), 20, 116
corporate social responsibility
(CSR), 162, 168, 169, 191
counter bids, 164

Dalal Street, 5
Darwin, Charles, 202
Das, Tarun, xxi, 7, 20, 23, 32, 71,
79, 116, 131, 132, 170, 172, 219
Datta, Partho, 101, 138, 144, 167,
170, 175
Delhi High Court, 157, 218
Deloitte, 37, 43, 44, 87, 101
Demonetization, 202
Dham, Vinod, 13
digital classrooms, 202
digital era, 202
'Direct from the Leadership'
campaign, 130
Directorate of Enforcement, 34
DLF, 15
Doshi, Bharath, 178
Durgashankar, S., 178, 179
Dutt, Barkha, 29

e-bulletin, 139
Economic Offences Wing, 118
Emergency Management and
Research Institute (EMRI), 67,
68, 69, 70, 71, 72, 168, 203, 205
emergency medical care, 67
employee stock option plans
(ESOP), 128, 198
Enron, 11, 59, 138, 187
Ernst & Young, 8, 14, 37
e-support password, 87

'expect the unexpected'
philosophy, 197
Expression of Interest (EOI), 159,
161, 162, 165, 181

FIFA-World Cup Football, 168
follow-up open auction, 166
Foreign Exchange Management
Act (FEMA), 34
forex, 14, 150
Full Life Cycle Leadership
initiative, 110

Gandhi, Mahatma, 205
Glaxo, 101
Goel, Anurag, 19, 103, 115, 171
Golden Peacock Award for
Corporate Excellence, 185
Goldman Sachs, 88, 90, 154, 159,
170, 175
Govind, Venugopal C., 176
GSK, 84, 136
Gupta, Prem Chand, 9, 19
Gupta, Rajat, 72, 158
Gupta, V.S.P., 39

hard infrastructure, 14
Harvard Business School, 177
HDFC, 116, 148, 149, 156, 174,
219
Health Management and Research
Institute (HMRI 104), 70
HelpAge India, 219
High Court of Andhra Pradesh, 34
House of Murugappa, 101
Hussey, Christopher, 211

IDBI, 84, 88, 91, 100, 115, 146,
148, 149, 150, 215, 219
'I-Me-My-Mine' syndrome, 196

Income Tax Department, 35, 41, 91, 119, 148, 217
India Asset Recovery Fund, 173
Indian Penal Code, 186
Indian Premier League (IPL), 164, 166, 174
Indian School of Business (ISB), 13, 18, 72
In-house Adjudication Mechanism (IAM), 194
insider corporate governance model, 188
Insolvency and Bankruptcy Code, 2016 (IBC), 194
Institute of Chartered Accountants of India (ICAI), xvii, 20, 21, 23, 30, 42, 45, 85, 96, 116, 141, 218
intellectual property (IP) rights, 157
Intranet (Satyam World), 131
Investor Education Protection Fund (IEPF), 191
IT assets, 14
ITC Grand Kakatiya, 156

Jayaraman, G., 4, 14, 179, 216, 221
job-hopping, 110
Joyce, Simon, 158
justice-delivery mechanism, 188

Kaliaropoulos, Peter, 97
Kamath, K.V., 71
Karnik, Kiran, xxi, 7, 19, 20, 21, 32, 71, 116, 130, 132, 170, 172, 219
Khusrokhan, Homi, 101, 138, 167, 170, 175
KPMG, 37, 43, 44, 101
Kroll, 163
Kurukshetra war, 206

Lakshminarayana, Vasagiri Venkata, 118
Larsen & Toubro (L&T), 89, 90, 163, 165, 170, 172, 173, 174
Lashkar-e-Taiba, xxv
Lawrence Sucharow, 102
Leaders Call, 176
Lehman Brothers, 10, 196
Lewinsky, Monica, 138
Life Insurance Corporation of India (LIC), xvii, 23, 116, 172, 219
Lord Krishna, 206

Madhapur, 31, 109
Madoff, 187
Mahindra, Anand, viii, xix, 177, 216
Mahindra & Mahindra, 174, 178, 179, 219
Mahindra Satyam, 11, 213, 215, 218
Mahindra Satyam Family, 213
Mahindra takeover, 180
Mainak, S. Balakrishna, 7, 23, 32, 116, 172
Malegam, Y.H., 176
Mallya, M.D., 149
Mayan mythology, 186
Maytas Infra, 13, 14, 15
Maytas Properties, 13, 14, 15, 16, 18
McGee, Dennis W., 142
McKenzie, Hamish, 142
Ministry of Corporate Affairs (MCA), 7, 9, 19, 20, 21, 22, 23, 35, 86, 102, 115, 116, 179, 186, 191
Mittal, Som, 9, 176
motivation measures, 139

Mukherjee, Pranab, 215
Mynampati, Ram, 13, 37

Narayan, Jayaprakash, 72
National Association of Software and Service Companies (NASSCOM), 9, 19, 110, 116, 176
National Australia Bank (NAB), 136, 141, 142
National Financial Reporting Authority (NFRA), 191
National Security Guard, xxv
National Stock Exchange, 4
Nayyar, Vineet, 165, 179, 216
Nehru, Jawaharlal, 211
Nestlé, 42, 142, 176
New Mangalore Port Trust, 120
News Cast (News Today Live), 131
New York Stock Exchange (NYSE), 7, 37, 89
Nifty, 85
Nomination and Remuneration Committee (NRC), 192, 193
Non-Disclosure Agreement, 159, 163

Obama, Barack, 78
online banking, 202
open bidding, 164, 166, 174
Oracle, 140, 171
outsider model, 188, 189

Palepu, Krishna, Dr, 13, 16, 18, 71
Palkhivala, Nani, 185
pandemic, xxii, 202
Parasaran, K., 155
Parekh, Deepak, xxi, 7, 19, 20, 21, 22, 32, 116, 130, 132, 135, 170, 172, 219

Patil, Pratibha Devisingh, 214
Piroj, Sam, Justice, 155
Prevention of Money Laundering Act, 34, 216
Process Confidentiality Agreement, 159, 163

Rajagopalachari, C., 211
Raju, Krishnam, 72
Raju, Rama, 13
Raju, Ramalinga, xvii, 4, 5, 8, 9, 13, 47, 53, 59, 60, 65, 67, 70, 71, 72, 104, 200, 206, 218
Rammohan Rao, M., Professor, 13
Rangineni, Vijay, 77, 104
Reddy, Raj, Prof., 72
Registrar of Companies (RoC), 12, 34, 103
remote sensing, 202
request for proposal (RFP), 159, 161, 181
Reserve Bank of India (RBI), 20
Richard, Henry, 12
Rights Offer, 155
Rosaiah, Konijeti, 70

Sahara, 21, 32, 191
Sahara India Financial Corporation Limited, 21
Saradha, 191
Sarbanes-Oxley Act, 187
Satti, Srinivasu, 14, 103
Satyam Computer Services Limited, 4
Satyam Foundation, 70, 71, 168
Satyam Infocity, 13, 31, 32, 213
Satyam Leadership Council, 46
Satyam Learning Center (SLC), 110, 111
Satyam–NAB relationship, 142

INDEX

Satyam School of Leadership (SSL), 110, 111
Satyam Technology Center (STC), 31, 109, 146, 213
Scotiabank, 136
sealed-cover bidding, 166
SEBI LODR, 187, 191
SEBI Takeover Regulations, 154, 155
Securities and Exchange Board of India (SEBI), 4, 7, 9, 14, 19, 44, 53, 54, 82, 85, 90, 91, 103, 115, 118, 122, 123, 154, 155, 156, 159, 162, 163, 166, 167, 172, 185, 187, 191, 193, 218, 219
Securities and Exchange Commission, 6, 84
Securities Appellate Tribunal, 19, 218
Sensex, 85
Serious Fraud Investigation Office (SFIO), 38, 103, 118, 192, 193, 217
Sharma, Manohar Lal, 157
Shroff, Pallavi, 33, 36, 91, 158, 170, 175
Shroff, Shardul S., 33, 36, 91, 102, 170, 175
Singapore, xxii, 147, 202
Singh, Manmohan, xxv, 98, 179, 215
Skilling, Jeffrey, 59
software telecom, 173
Sotheby auction, 164
'Source', 139
Spice Group, 163, 164

Standstill Agreement, 159, 163
state Crime Branch, 38
strategic investors, 90, 150, 157
Supreme Court, 155, 160, 216, 217, 218
'Surf the Board' campaign, 132

Takeover Code, 85
Tech Mahindra, xxiii, 163, 165, 170, 172, 173, 174, 175, 176, 177, 178, 179, 180, 181, 215, 216, 217, 219, 220, 221
Tendulkar, Sachin, 197
the Satyam Learning Center, 110
the School of Leadership, 110

Upaid, 86, 103, 121, 157, 158, 188, 215
US Securities Act, 163
Utla, Balaji, Dr, 70

Vadlamani, Srinivas, 13
Venturbay Consultants Private Limited, 173

white knight, 153
WL Ross & Co, 163, 165, 173
Wolters, Marco Peter, 96
work from home, 202
WorldCom, 11, 187
writ petition, 157, 218

Xerox, 187

Yelloji, Naveen, 71
YouTube, 130, 131

www.ingramcontent.com/pod-product-compliance
Lightning Source LLC
Chambersburg PA
CBHW031425150426
43191CB00006B/398